CB078524

# Pathway to Grammar

## Student's Book

# 4

Richmond

Richmond
58 St Aldates
Oxford
OX1 1ST
United Kingdom

*Pathway to Grammar Student's Book Level 4*

First Edition: 2015
Seventh Reprint: January 2023
ISBN: 978-607-06-1095-0


Av. Río Mixcoac No. 274, Col. Acacias,
Benito Juárez, C.P. 03240, Ciudad de México

Publisher: Justine Piekarowicz
Editorial Team: Jennifer S. Li, Joep van der Werff
Art and Design Coordinator: Marisela Pérez
Design: Erika Martínez
Layout: Daniel Mejía
Pre-Press Coordinator: Daniel Santillán
Pre-Press Team: Susana Alcántara, Virginia Arroyo
Cover Design: Erika Martínez

Cover Photograph: ©**THINKSTOCK:** iStock (alan64, hxdyl); Polka Dot

Illustrations: Erick Arellano pp. 8, 28, 48, 52, 66; Sheila Cabeza de Vaca pp. 7, 12, 26, 30, 47, 49, 65; Guadalupe Calvo pp. 15, 37, 57, 59, 76, 81; Gilberto Guzmán pp. 19, 38; Sebastian Hernández pp. 16, 56, 60, 77, 82; Luis Montiel pp. 5, 9, 25, 29, 46, 51, 67, 69; Alma Nuñez pp. 35, 55, 58, 75, 78; Edgardo Solas pp. 6, 10, 27, 31, 45, 50, 68; Ismael Vázquez p. 82

Photographs: ⓒ NASA p. 83; ©**REPOSITORIO:** Ediciones Santillana, S.A. (Argentina) pp. 13, 21, 30, 43, 49; Santillana de Ediciones, S.A. (Bolivia) p. 49; Santillana Educación S.L. pp. 21 (Amador Toril Díaz), 43 (Marisa Ortega), 59 (SERIDEC PHOTOIMAGENES CD, S.L.); ©**RICHMOND ARCHIVE:** p. 80; ©**THINKSTOCK:** AbleStock.com pp. 11 (Hemera Technologies), 47 (Hemera Technologies); amanaimagesRF p. 56 (amanaimagesRF); Blend Images p. 20 (Jon Feingersh); Creatas pp. 10 (Jupiterimages, Creatas Images), 14 (Jupiterimages), 38 (Creatas Images), 62 (Creatas), 76 (Creatas Images, Jupiterimages),82 (Jupiterimages); Digital Vision pp. 4 (Michael Blann), 24 (Michael Blann), 34 (Michael Blann), 36 (Noel Hendrickson), 39 (Donald Miralle), 44 (Digital Vision), 54 (Digital Vision), 70 (Darrin Klimek); Eyecandy Images p. 62 (Eyecandy Images); Fuse pp. 74 (Fuse), 76 (Fuse); Goodshoot pp. 42 (Goodshoot), 45 (Goodshoot), 77 (Goodshoot); Hemera pp. (Sergey Volkov), 14 (Benis Arapovic), 21 (Eric IsselTe), 24 (Mikhail Kokhanchikov, Johan Knelsen), 34 (Benis Arapovic), 39 (Laurent Renault), 39 (Elena Elisseeva), 44 (Glen Jones), 67 (Robert Wilson), 74 (Sergej Petrakov), 77 (Cathy Yeulet), 79 (Ovchynnikov Igor); Ingram Publishing pp. 47 (Ingram Publishing), 71 (Ingram Publishing); iStock pp. 3-83 (Ociacia), (suksao999), 4 (Feverpitched, garth11, lanych, kimberrywood, studio7, mbot, cherezoff, PIKSEL, A_teen, Alliance, khwanchais, tuja66, ATIC12, alzajac, Piotr Przeszlo, leolintang), 6 (Artranq, XiXinXing, IuriiSokolov, fotokostic, konmesa), 7 (waldru, Enskanto, Michal Bryc, Atthapol Saita), 9 (gemenacom, OverShoot), 10 (Dean Mitchell, monkeybusinessimages, Muralinath, shironosov), 12 (SergiyN), 13 (Donhype, Wetzkaz, monkeybusinessimages, SerrNovik), 14 (Isabelle_C, karayuschij, Ljupco, archideaphoto, piyathep, anneleven, kojihirano, AnnaDudek, sputnikos, Eric Isselée, alan64, SerrNovik, Dirima, eyewave, saiva, sumnersgraphicsinc, soleg, Wojciech Gajda, Bahadirkar, Sergiy Trofimov), 15 (monkeybusinessimages), 16 (Sashkinw), 17 (CoreyFord, Krivinis, james steidl, Robert Churchill, vichie81, Maksym Bondarchuk, sputnikos), 18 (Musat, abadonian, Eric Isselée, tellmemore000, miblue5, JudyDillon, Lennon_Schneider, JaysonPhotography, savetrev, Vacclav), 19 (amwu), 20 (iofoto), 21 (sommail, kobelev, GlobalP, DJSrki, Anna Davydova, karammiri), 22 (Liufuyu, M_a_y_a, Freeartist), 23 (alexis84), 24 (SBphotographer, tuja66, akinshin, Lusoimages, tuja66, HudRuk, ClaudioVentrella, Gajus, AndreyPopov, ArtGapan, jclegg, Eren Dündar, tuja66, Mike_Pellinni, KeremYucel, mmpile), 26 (MikeyGen73, fotofermer, mathieu boivin, Hyrma, davide chiarito, fotofermer, 3DMaster, rtguest), 27 (Harvepino, tuja66, nabihariahi, tuja66, Oleksiy Mark, Lusoimages), 28 (IvonneW), 30 (Ken Drysdale, MarinaMariya, insima), 31 (monkeybusinessimages, froxx, Березняков Андрей, danr13), 32 (WilleeCole, GlobalP, Elena Butinova, cynoclub, Eric Isselée, Iakov Filimonov, Smileus), 33 (YanLev, Frizzantine, OcusFocus), 34 (adisa, Ljupco, Suljo, enisaksoy, archideaphoto, Alias-Ching, Issaurinko, Alliance, khwanchais, Liv Friis-Larsen, KocherginDA, Igor Vesninov, SergiyN, destillat, phasinphoto, iStock, _ba_, Zvozdochka, XiXinXing, Renee Keith, Jani Bryson), 36 (-aniaostudio-, Okea, Victoire_Lefevre), 38 (Joan Kimball, xavigm, vladj55), 39 (Jani Bryson, XiXinXing), 40 (gemenacom, Jean-nicolas Nault), 41 (Sashkinw, C-You, Picsfive, nito100, Jan Hanus, Danish Khan, Yingko, Olga Popova, ISerg), 42 (feedough, Jaren Wicklund, aragami123345, Carther), 44 (Moma7, KatarzynaBialasiewicz, Igor Mojzes, VALPAZOU, gbh007, psphotograph, iStock, monkeybusinessimages, digitalgenetics, Alliance, Hlib Shabashnyi, b-d-s, ATIC12), 45 (furtaev, Jill Chen), 47 (Kati Neudert, Tara McCray), 48 (Agnieszka Gaul), 49 (gangliu10, Mark Herreid, Igor Mojzes), 53 (Nerthuz, igorshi, Alexander Bedrin, prapann, scanrail, antpkr, stsmhn, kvkirillov, pigphoto, hkeita, odmeyer, Wacharaphong, Believe_In_Me, kuarmungadd, Dirk Ott, mshch, Aneese, 3DSculptor), 56 (shironosov, LuckyToBeThere, Dgwildlife, sirichai_raksue, riksphotography), 58 (alexis84, BrianAJackson, wavebreakmedia), 59 (Urs Siedentop, fotofermer, ekinyalgin, czekma13), 61 (Sashkinw, deyangeorgiev, Pavel Losevsky, hxdyl, Erdal Bayhan, Torresigner), 62 (gawriloff, wojciech_gajda), 64 (Peshkova, FooTToo, Katarzyna Bialasiewicz, belchonock, nevodka, kreinick, Maxim Blinkov, IPGGutenbergUKLtd, stu99, aijohn784, VYCHEGZHANINA, poligonchik, archideaphoto), 67 (kzenon, panasw, Roman Okopny), 70 (marcduf, TNTbomb_dot_com, cthomas888, miflippo, Steve Mcsweeny), 72 (dianazh, belchonock, olgna, kumakuma1216), 73 (IPGGutenbergUKLtd, Jacek Chabraszewski), 74 (Lyudmila Suvorova, vetkit, Carsten Reisinger, uuurska, iStock, ayzek, Yuko Hirao, tetmc, cj2a, GlobalP, Svetlana Valuyskaya), 76 (Beaubizz, monkeybusinessimages), 77 (crazydiva, Jannoon028, Piotr Krześlak, pilipphoto), 78 (morningmagenta, Melinda Schneider, Michael Green, kinemero, mgreen2007, Nick Hayes), 79 matsilvan, panic_attack, iStock), 82 (tab1962), 84 (iStock, Sashkinw), 85 (iStock), 86 (iStock), 87 (iStock), 88 (iStock), 89 (iStock), 91 (iStock); iStock Editorial pp. 20 (mjbs), 67 (BaroneFi, trekandshoot, stevezmina1); Keith Levit Photography p. 4 (Keith Levit); liquidlibrary pp. 14 (Jupiterimages), 45 (Jupiterimages); Monkey Business pp. 31 (Monkey Business Images), 64 (Monkey Business Images Ltd); moodboard pp. 4 (moodboard), 34 (moodboard), 45 (Mike Watson Images), 70 (moodboard), 72 (moodboard), 76 (moodboard); Photodisc pp. 4 (Photodisc, Digital Vision), 13 (Medioimages/Photodisc), 20 (Photodisc), 24 (Digital Vision), 27 (Digital Vision, Ryan McVay), 36 (Noel Hendrickson), 39 (Barry Austin Photography), 42 (Jack Hollingsworth), 54 (Digital Vision), 58 (Digital Vision), 62 (Digital Vision), 64 (Digital Vision), 73 (James Woodson), 78 (Apple Tree House); PhotoObjects.net pp. 24 (Hemera Technologies), 64 (Photos.com), 78 (Hemera Technologies); Photos.com p. 30 (Photos.com); Pixland p. 13 (Pixland); Polka Dot p. 58 (Jupiterimages); Purestock pp. 6 (Purestock), 11 (Purestock), 54 (Purestock), 56 (Purestock), 76 (Purestock); Randy Faris/Fuse p. 76 (Randy Faris/Fuse); Ron Chapple Studios p. 54 (Ron Chapple Stock); Stockbyte pp. 10 (Comstock), 18 (Comstock Images), 34 (Jupiterimages), 36 (Stockbyte), 70 (Jupiterimages), 74 (Comstock Images, George Doyle), 77 (Stockbyte), 79 (Jupiterimages, Comstock Images); VStock p. 64 (Vstock LLC); Wavebreak Media pp. 14 (Wavebreakmedia Ltd), 22 (Wavebreakmedia Ltd), 24 (Wavebreakmedia Ltd), 27 (Wavebreakmedia Ltd), 47 (Wavebreakmedia Ltd); Zoonar p. 24 (Zoonar/unknown)



Printed in Brazil by Forma Certa

Lote: 774582
Código: 292710920

# Contents

# Unit 1

pets

aquariums

bird cages rabbit

dolphin

feed (*v*)

Internet

loudly (*adv*)

mistake

morning

evening

play tennis (*v*)

quickly (*adv*)

quietly (*adv*)

slowly (*adv*)

text (*v*)

# Simple present, affirmative

## 1 Write, look, and number.

Sally *wakes up* (*wake up*) at seven o'clock in the morning on Saturday.
She ______ [1] (*run*) for an hour, ______ [2] (*eat*) breakfast, and then
______ [3] (*take*) a shower. Sally works in an aquarium. She trains the dolphins.
She always ______ [4] (*ride*) her bike to the aquarium. Sally ______ [5] (*feed*)
the dolphins at ten. Sally and the dolphins ______ [6] (*have*) two shows on Saturdays.
After the shows, they ______ [7] (*swim*) together. In the evening, Sally ______ [8]
(*go*) home. [9]

☐ 

☐ 

☐ 

☐ 

☐ 

1 

☐ 

☐ 

☐ 

# Simple present, negative

F

**1 Look, match, and write. Use *don't* or *doesn't*.**

1 

2 

3 

4 

5 

6 

| | | | |
|---|---|---|---|
| My pet rabbit | My aunt | do my homework in the evening. | text in her car. |
| I | Dad | study English together. | use the Internet at work. |
| The three children | The two women | eat carrots. | play tennis in the morning. |

1. I *don't do my homework in the evening* ________.
2. The three children ________.
3. Dad ________.
4. My aunt ________.
5. The two women ________.
6. My pet rabbit ________.

# Simple present, interrogative

**1 Match.**

1. Do you use the Internet at school? — b
2. Does your mother cook on Sundays?
3. Does your brother text on his phone?
4. Do your cousins ride the bus in the morning?

a. No, she doesn't.
b. Yes, I do.
c. No, they don't.
d. Yes, he does.

**2 Look and write.**

1 

*Does it sit on the swing* ______?

*Yes, it does* ______.

2 

______ eat from a bowl?

No, it ______.

3 

______ climb on the cage?

______.

4 

______ fly in the sky?

______.

# Time expressions

## 1 Sort.

day | Wednesday | week | times a week
a week | times a month | a year | weekend
morning | times a year | evening | a month

**Once, twice...**

______________________
______________________
______________________

**Three, four...**

______________________
______________________
______________________

**Every...**

*day*
______________________
______________________
______________________
______________________
______________________

## 2 Read and rewrite.

1. Adam feeds his pet bird *on weekdays and weekends.*
   *Adam feeds his pet bird every day*.
2. Lori uses the Internet at the library *on Tuesdays and Wednesdays.*
   ______________________.
3. Jim and Gina clean the aquarium for their fish *every four weeks.*
   ______________________.
4. Henry walks his dog *on Mondays, Wednesdays, and Fridays.*
   ______________________.

# How often...?

## 1 Read and write.

| every day | every weekend | never | once a week | twice a week | three times a week |
|---|---|---|---|---|---|

### Paul's Pet Planner

**Monday**
feed pets, give birds fresh water
**Tuesday**
feed pets, give rabbit a carrot
**Wednesday**
feed pets, give birds fresh water
**Thursday**
feed pets, have play time with rabbit

**Friday**
feed pets, give birds fresh water
**Saturday**
feed pets, clean rabbit cage
**Sunday**
feed pets, clean bird cage, have play time with rabbit

1. *How often does* Paul give his rabbit a carrot? *Once a week*.
2. ________________ Paul feed his pets? ________________.
3. ________________ Paul and his rabbit have play time? ________________.
4. ________________ Paul clean the rabbit cage? ________________.
5. ________________ the birds get fresh water? ________________.
6. ________________ the pets play together? ________________.

## 2 Answer for yourself.

1. How often do you play with a pet? ________________.
2. How often do you clean your room? ________________.
3. How often do you play sports? ________________.

# Adverbs of manner 1

## 1 Match, look, and write.

| | | | | | |
|---|---|---|---|---|---|
| loud | good | careful | quietly | quick | happily |
| bad | slowly | happy | loudly | slow | quiet |
| well | sad | badly | carefully | sadly | quickly |

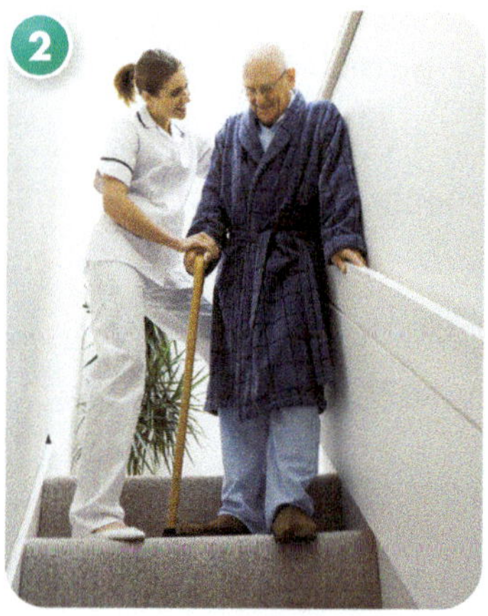

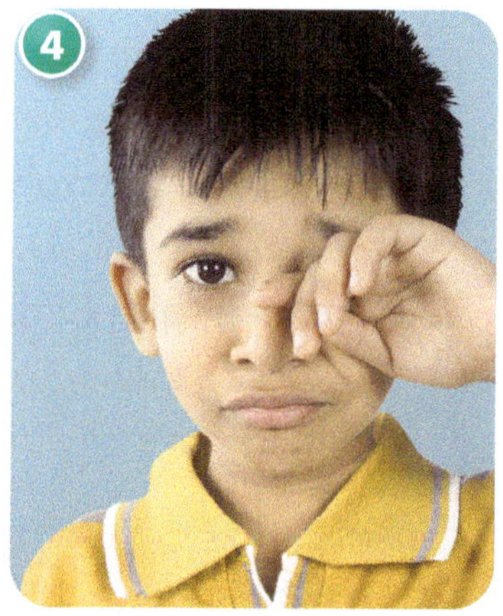

1. The opera singer sings very *well*.
2. The man is walking down the stairs __________.
3. Mina is riding her bike __________.
4. Jay is crying __________ because he lost the game.
5. People always talk __________ in the library.
6. The boys are behaving __________ in class.

## 2 Look, read, and write.

Mike

Mike likes adventure.
He ________ (*happy*) climbs tall mountains!
He goes mountain climbing twice a year.
He uses special equipment to climb ____________ (*careful*).

Nina and Meg like tennis.
They run ________ (*quick*) on the tennis court!
They play tennis every morning in the sports center.
They wear tennis skirts.
They play very ________ (*good*)!

Nina and Meg

## 3 Read again and write.

How often | What | When | Where | Who | Why

1. *What does Mike use to climb mountains* ? Special equipment.
2. ____________________ ? Twice a year.
3. ____________________ ? In the mountains.
4. ____________________ ? Because he likes adventure.
5. ____________________ ? Nina and Meg like tennis.
6. ____________________ ? In the morning.
7. ____________________ ? In the sports center.
8. ____________________ ? Tennis skirts.
9. ____________________ ? Because they love it!

## 1 Listen and write. 2

ADAM: Let's put on a show! We can work together.
Emily, what are you good at?

EMILY: I'm good at *painting pictures* ________.

JOHN: Yes, Emily paints very ____________________! She can make the set.

ADAM: That's great! Tim, what are you good at?

TIM: I'm good at ____________________. I can be an actor!

ADAM: I talk ____________________, but I'm good at ____________________.
I can do the sound and lights!

EMILY: How about our other friends? What are they good at?

ADAM: They're good at ____________________. They can be the audience!

set

actor

sound

audience

## 2 Read the dialogue with a friend.

## 3 Talk with a friend. Then write.

| jumping |
| --- |
| playing |
| reading |
| running |
| talking |
| writing |

A: __________, what are you good at?

B: I'm good at ____________________.
I __________ very __________.
What are you good at?

A: I'm good at ____________________.
I __________ very __________.

## Let's sing!

**1 Listen. Then number the pictures.** 3

### The Dream Team

1. We are a team as good as a dream.
   We're always together
2. In good and bad weather.

3. Once a day we loudly play
4. Every night we quietly fight.

5. Twice a year we shed a tear
6. When dolphins sing badly
   And we listen sadly.

7. Sometimes it's a blast to run very fast
8. And often it's swell to jump very well.
   Every weekend we happily send
9. A birthday card to our favorite friend.

3

1

5

# Unit 2

annoying

cloudy

cold

comfortable

dangerous

deep

dry

expensive

fat

funny

hot

pretty

strong

sunny

thin

wet

# As ... as for the same 4

As ... as = the same

## 1 Follow and write the opinions.

| | | | |
|---|---|---|---|
| 1 | lions | intelligent | elephants |
| 2 | soccer | important | basketball |
| 3 | bicycle | big | car |
| 4 | boys | interesting | girls |
| 5 | English | expensive | math |

1. *Lions aren't as big as elephants*.
2. *Soccer is as* .
3. .
4. .
5. .

## 2 Look and write.

1. *happy*

   *Jay is as happy as Rob*.
2. *short*

   .
3. *tall*

   .

# Comparative adjectives, -er

## 1 Sort by ending type.

cloudier colder deeper drier fatter hotter newer
prettier sadder shorter slower sunnier uglier wetter

stronger ___________ ___________ ___________ ___________ ___________
thinner ___________ ___________ ___________ ___________ ___________
funnier ___________ ___________ ___________ ___________ ___________

## 2 Write, look, and mark true (*T*) or false (*F*).

| Monday | Tuesday | Wednesday | Thursday | Friday |
|---|---|---|---|---|
|  |  |  |  |  |
| 55°F (12°C) | 60°F (16°C) | 65°F (18°C) | 60°F (16°C) | 55°F (12°C) |

1. Monday was *colder than* (*cold*) Tuesday. (T) F
2. Friday was ____________ (*wet*) Wednesday. T F
3. Thursday was ____________ (*cloudy*) Friday. T F
4. Thursday was ____________ (*sunny*) Wednesday. T F

## 3 Write and draw the weather where you are.

1. Today is ______________________ yesterday.
2. Yesterday was ______________________ today.

| Today |
|---|
| Yesterday |

## Comparative adjectives, *more / less*

**1 Look and circle.**

1. The red car is ***less*** / ***more*** comfortable than the blue car.
2. The blue car is ***less*** / ***more*** boring than the red car.
3. The red car is ***less*** / ***more*** expensive than the blue car.
4. The red car is ***less*** / ***more*** modern than the blue car.

**2 Look, match, and write.**

*modern*
*expensive*
*comfortable*
*elegant*
*beautiful*

1. The chair is more modern than the sofa.
2. ______________________________.
3. ______________________________.
4. ______________________________.
5. ______________________________.

# Superlative adjectives, *-est*

## 1 Look and write.

big clean deep dry heavy long tall

1

2

3

4

5

6

7

1. Whales are *the heaviest* ________ animals in the sea.
2. The Nile is ________________ river in the world.
3. The Atacama Desert is ________________ place on Earth.
4. From 1931 to 1972, the Empire State Building was ________________ building in New York.
5. Iguazu Falls is one of ________________ waterfalls of all.
6. Iceland is ________________ country in the world.
7. The Pacific Ocean is ________________ ocean of all.

# Superlative adjectives, *most*

## 1 Match and write the opinions.

| | | |
|---|---|---|
| English is | the most beautiful | place at home. |
| Sushi is | the most expensive | animals in the wild. |
| My bedroom is | the most comfortable | food of all. |
| Diamonds are | the most delicious | snake in our country. |
| Lions are | the most interesting | subject of all. |
| The rattlesnake is | the most dangerous | jewels of all. |

1. *English is the most interesting subject of all* ________________.
2. ________________________________________.
3. ________________________________________.
4. ________________________________________.
5. ________________________________________.
6. ________________________________________.

## 2 Write about yourself and draw yourself.

1. I'm the ____________ student in my class. 2. I'm ____________ person in my family.

# Comparative and superlative of *good, bad*

good → better → the best  bad → worse → the worst

## 1 Read and circle.

1. My best friend Elizabeth is ***the best*** / ***better*** student in our school.
2. My grades are usually ***worse*** / ***bad*** than hers.
3. But this week, my grade on the test was just as ***good*** / ***better*** as Elizabeth's!
4. My brother Dan is always ***worse*** / ***the worst*** dancer at the party.
5. But he doesn't want to be a ***best*** / ***better*** dancer.
6. He thinks ***bad*** / ***worst*** dancing is ***funny*** / ***funnier*** than ***best*** / ***good*** dancing!

## 2 Think and write.

1. The best book of all is ______________________.
2. The worst movie of all is ______________________.
3. ______________ are better pets than ______________.
4. ______________ weather is better than ______________ weather.

## 3 Look and write.

as big as   big   bigger than   the biggest

1. The rabbit *is as big as* ____________ the cat.
2. The rabbit and the cat are ____________ the mouse.
3. The dog ____________ animal of all.

as comfortable as   more / less comfortable than   the most comfortable

4. The chairs are ____________ the bed.
5. The sofa ____________ the chairs.
6. The bed ____________ of all.

## 4 Think and write.

as delicious as   more / less delicious than   the most delicious

1. Ice cream ____________ cookies.
2. Lollipops ____________ ice cream.
3. Chocolate ____________ of all.

Let's talk!

**1 Listen and write.** 5

MOM: I think the city is the ___best___ place for a vacation!

DAD: Really? I know cities have interesting restaurants and museums, but they're the most ____________!

MOM: That's true. I know the beach is less ____________ than the city, and I think it's more ____________.

JANE: But I think the beach isn't as ____________ as the city. It's the ____________ place of all on a sunny day!

DAD: I think a vacation at home is the best. It's ____________ expensive than the beach or the city. We all know it's the most ____________ place to be!

**2 Read the dialogue with a friend.**

**3 Talk with a friend. Then write.**

A: What do you think? Where is the best place to visit?

B: I think ____________ is the best place.
I think / know it has ____________.
What do you think?

A: I think ____________ is better than ____________.
I think / know it has ____________.

## Let's sing!

**1** Listen and circle. 6

| hot<br>hotter<br>hottest |
|---|
| long<br>longer<br>longest |
| slow<br>slower<br>slowest |
| wet<br>wetter<br>wettest |

### Amazing Things

The most interesting thing on the land, the most amazing thing in the air,
The most beautiful thing in the sea, come and learn about them with me!

England is ____________,
Brazil is ____________,
But India is the ____________ place of all.

Cancun is ____________,
Panama is ____________,
But Libya is the ____________ place of all.

The sea horse is ____________,
The turtle is ____________,
But the snail is the ____________ creature of all.

Cobras are ____________,
Boas are ____________,
But anacondas are the ____________ snakes of all.

**2** Now draw four illustrations.

# Unit 3

bottle

cans

DVD player

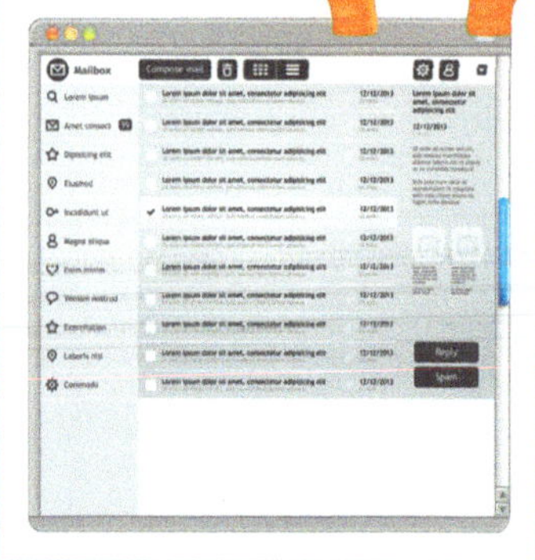

e-mail

(french) fries

go camping (*v*)

grass

grown-ups

lake

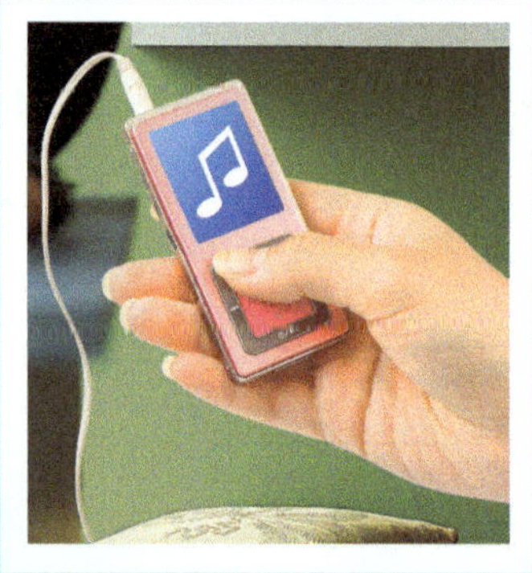

MP3 player

pasta

popcorn

rainbow

river

sand

waterfall

# There was, There were

There was a lot of bread. = uncountable nouns
There were a lot of sandwiches. = countable nouns

## 1 Read, color, and write.

| a little | a lot of | one | six | some | three |
|---|---|---|---|---|---|

1. *There were three* ______ gray waterfalls above the lake.
2. *There was a lot of* ______ blue water in the lake.
3. ______ green trees near the lake.
4. ______ brown grass under the trees.
5. ______ yellow sand next to the lake.
6. ______ beautiful rainbow across the lake.

# There wasn't, There weren't

There **wasn't** any **juice**. = uncountable nouns
There **weren't** any **bananas**. = countable nouns

## 1 Look and write.

1. *There weren't any* ______ fries.
2. *There wasn't any* ______ soda.
3. ______________________ hot dogs.
4. ______________________ water.
5. ______________________ popcorn.
6. ______________________ hamburgers.

## 2 Write and draw.

Last ______________________, I went to a restaurant. I liked the menu a lot!
There weren't ______________________.
There wasn't ______________________.
But there was ______________________,
and there were ______________________!

# Was there...? Were there...?

Was there any sand? = uncountable nouns
Were there any sandcastles? = countable nouns

## 1 Look and write.

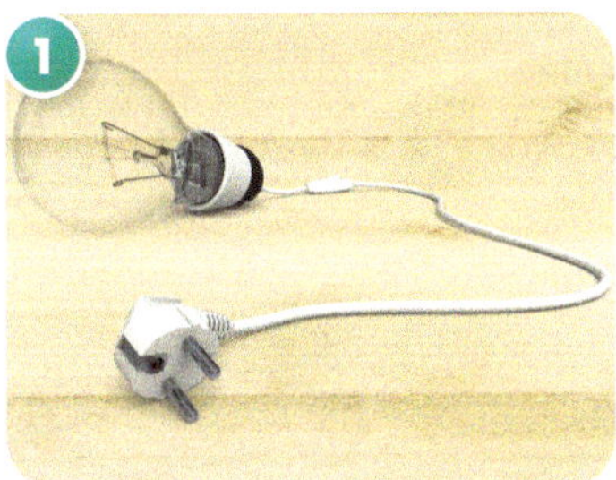

electric power 1879

calculator 1969

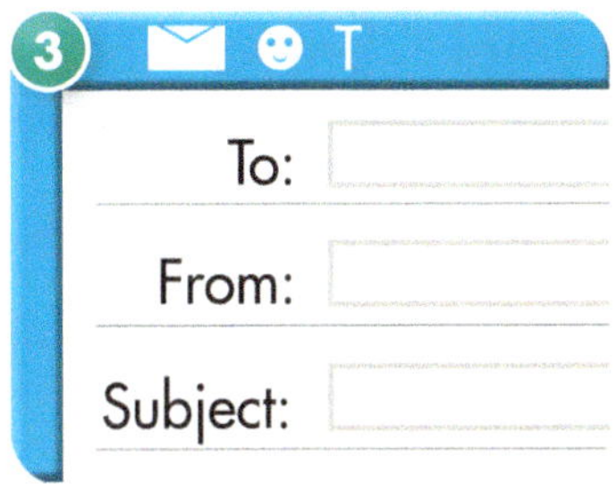


e-mail 1971

CD 1972

personal computer 1974

Internet 1993

DVD player 1995

MP3 player 1998

1. *Was there any* electric power in 1850? *No, there wasn't*.
2. ________ calculators in 1965? ________.
3. ________ e-mails in 1990? ________.
4. ________ CDs in 1925? ________.
5. ________ personal computers in 1980? ________.
6. ________ Internet in 1945? ________.
7. ________ DVD players in 1970? ________.
8. ________ MP3 players in 1950? ________.

# How much...? How many...? 7

How **much**...? = uncountable nouns
How **many**...? = countable nouns

## 1 Read and sort.

apples boxes of cereal bread cheese cookies water

**How much?** *bread* ____________ ____________

**How many?** ____________ ____________ ____________

## 2 Look, circle, and write.

1. How (**much**) / **many** rice *was there*? *There was a lot of rice*.
2. How **much** / (**many**) bottles of juice *were there*? *There were two bottles*.
3. How **much** / **many** milk ____________? ____________.
4. How **much** / **many** oranges ____________? ____________.
5. How **much** / **many** bags of pasta ____________? ____________.
6. How **much** / **many** salad ____________? ____________.
7. How **much** / **many** cans of soup ____________? ____________.

# Used to

## 1 Look and write.

drive a car | jump rope | play baseball | ride a bike | ride a horse | stay up late

**They're grown-ups now, but when they were younger…**

1. *When she was younger, Aunt Kate used to stay up late*.
2. *When she was younger, Grandma* __________.
3. __________.
4. __________.
5. __________.
6. __________.

## Didn't use to

**1 Look and mark true (*T*) or false (*F*).**

**Two hundred years ago...**

1. ...people used to go to the movies. T (F)
2. ...people used to play the violin. T F
3. ...people used to travel by plane. T F
4. ...women used to wear jeans. T F
5. ...people used to ride horses. T F
6. ...people used to write e-mails. T F

**2 Now correct the false sentences.**

*People didn't use to go to the movies*_______________.

_______________________________________________.

_______________________________________________.

_______________________________________________.

# *Use to*, interrogative

## 1 Look and write.

Yes, I did. No, I didn't.

use to used to

COACH DAN: Welcome to Camp Woods! You'll love it here. It's the same as when I was a boy!

BRETT: Did you *use to* ___________ go camping here when you were young?

COACH DAN: *Yes, I did* ___________! My brother and I ___________ go every year. We were younger than you are now.

BRETT: Did you ___________ swim in the river?

COACH DAN: ___________.

BRETT: Did you ___________ call your mom on your cell phone at night?

COACH DAN: ___________! People didn't have cell phones then. I ___________ call my mom from a pay phone!

## 2 Write and answer for yourself.

1. When you were little, did you use to go camping? ___________________
2. When you were little, did you use to use a cell phone? ___________________

Let's talk!

## 1 Listen and write. 8

cat cub lion kitten rabbit

ZOOKEEPER: This ___lion___ is very big and strong now. But he used to be small!
A baby __________ is called a __________. This __________ used to play all the time. But now he sleeps a lot!

ALEX BLACK: He's just like my __________! She didn't use to sleep all day. She used to play all the time when she was a baby.

ZOOKEEPER: Do you know what a baby __________ is called?

ALEX BLACK: A baby __________ is called a __________.

ZOOKEEPER: Yes! Did you know that baby __________ are called __________, too?

## 2 Read the dialogue with a friend.

## 3 Talk with a friend. Then write.

A: What is a ______________ called when it's a baby?

B: A baby ______________ is called a ______________.

A: Yes! That ______________ used to ______________.

It didn't use to ______________.

## Let's sing!

**1 Write. Then listen and check.** 9

### Life Used to Be So Good

I used to go_____ to the beach.
I used to p_____ in the sand,
I used to s_____ in the sea,
My friends used to g_____ with me.

I used to do it, but now I don't.
Life used to b_____ so good!
I used to do it, but now I don't.
This year I really should!

I used to s_____ in hotels,
They used to h_____ a big pool.
I used to lie in the sun,
I used to h_____ lots of fun.

I used to s_____ the big waves.
I used to c_____ white shells,
I used to s_____ in a boat,
Now it all seems so remote.

# Unit 4

coat

dry (*v*) wash (*v*)

holiday

hungry (*adj*)

invite (*v*)

pajamas

play a sport (*v*)

put on (*v*)

rain (*n, v*)

1 scarf, 2 scarves

snow (*n, v*)

sweater

swimsuits

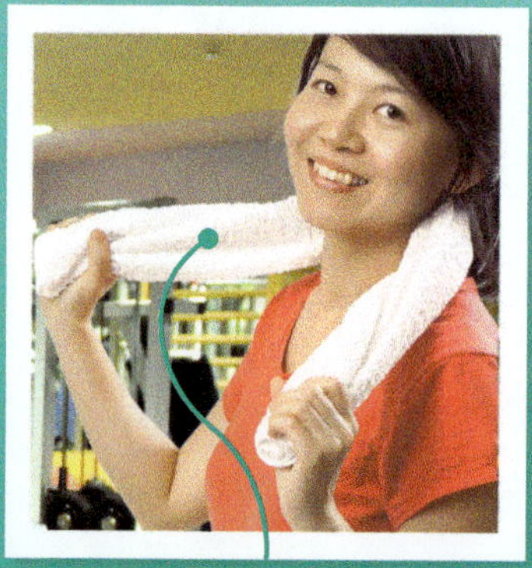

towel

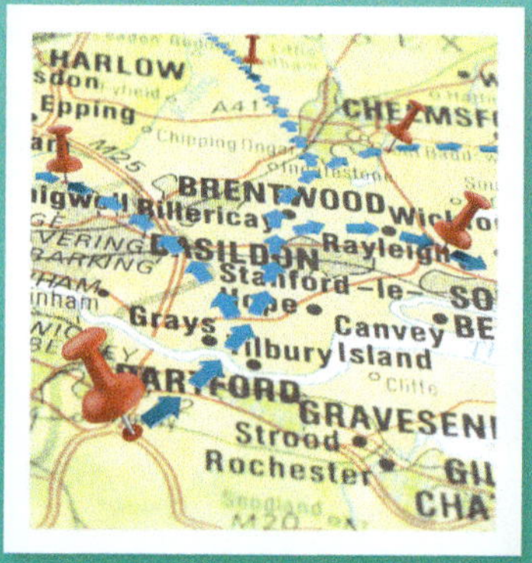


travel (*v*)

## Simple past

regular verbs = verb + *ed* (climbed);
irregular verbs = irregular form (give → gave)

### 1 Match.

drink fall go have make put on wear

fell drank made put on wore went had

### 2 Read and write.

Last Friday it __snowed__ (*snow*), so there was a holiday. We ________ (*don't go*) to school. We ________ (*play*) in the snow! First, we ________ (*put on*) our winter clothes. I ________ (*wear*) a scarf, a sweater, and a hat. My sister ________ (*have*) a big coat. In the morning, we ________ (*fall*) back into the snow and ________ (*make*) "snow angels!" But we ________ (*don't skate*) on the lake because the ice was too thin. In the evening, we were cold, so we ________ (*go*) inside and ________ (*drink*) hot chocolate. It was a great day!

# Using different tenses 10

I washed the dishes yesterday.
My brother is washing the dishes now.
Our parents are going to wash the dishes tomorrow.



## 1 Read and circle.

 = yesterday  = today (now)  = tomorrow

| | |
|---|---|
| They cleaned the windows. | He's feeding his pet rabbit. |
| It's going to rain. | We invited our friends to a party. |
| She's wearing a new coat. | They're going to paint the house. |
| You bought a video game. | We're baking a cake. |
| He's going to kick the ball. | He bought pajamas with blue stripes. |
| She's fishing on a boat in the ocean. | She's going to go visit a friend. |

## 2 Read and rewrite.

1. They played basketball last week.
   *They're playing basketball* right now.
   *They're going to play basketball* next Tuesday.
2. Erica's going to fly to France in February.
   ______________________ when she was six.
   ______________________ right now.
3. I'm throwing out the trash right now.
   ______________________ tomorrow morning.
   ______________________ last night.

Practice with the Pathway to Certification app!

## 3 Look and write.

1. Yesterday Sharon ______________ (*invite*) all her friends to a party.
2. Now they ______________ (*eat*) birthday cake.
3. Soon they ______________ (*go swimming*) in the pool.

4. Sue and Tim ______________ (*wake up*) very early this morning.
5. They ______________ (*drive*) to the airport now.
6. They ______________ (*arrive*) in Cancun in an hour.

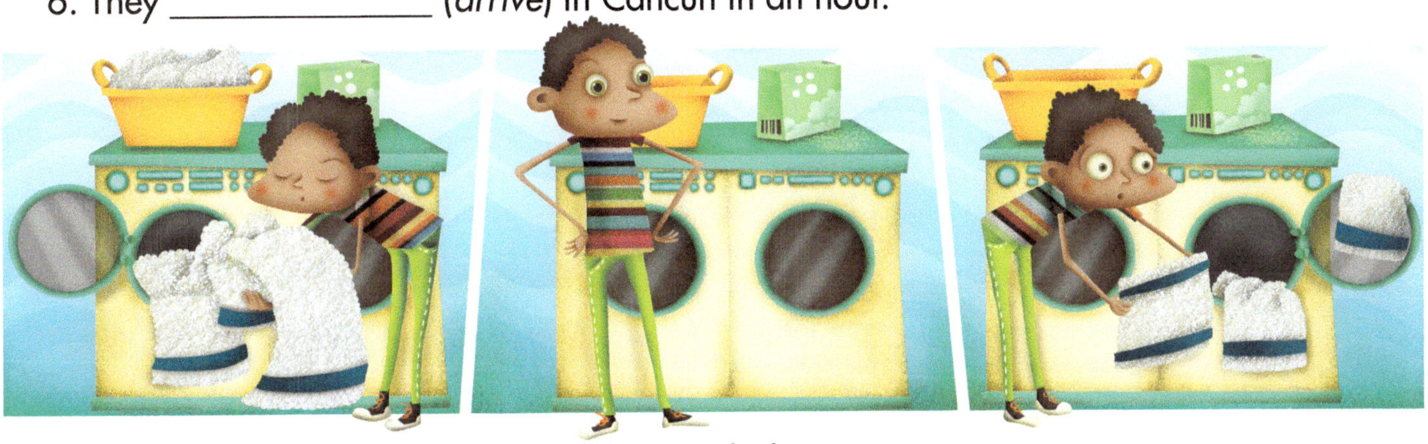

7. Peter ______________ (*wash*) all his towels this morning.
8. Now he ______________ (*dry*) his towels for a very long time.
9. He ______________ (*buy*) all new towels at the mall this afternoon.

# Conjunctions *and, or, but*

## 1 Look and write.

and but or

1 VENDOR: Would you like chocolate ___*or*___ vanilla ice cream?

2 GIRL: Mommy, I'm hungry! I want popcorn ______ a soda right now!

3 BOY: Your character can run ______ jump. He can't do both at the same time!

4 MOM: You washed the dog, ______ you didn't dry her!

## 2 Write about yourself.

I usually like eating __________ or __________ for dinner,
___*but*___ tonight we're going to eat __________ and __________.

# Conjunction *because*

**1 Look, read, and write.**

1. Why is the man wearing a uniform? *Because he's* ______________________.
2. Why are the people cheering? ______________________.

**2 Look and write.**

buy   fall   laugh   smile   take

1 

2 

3 

1. She's *laughing because she fell on the ice*.
2. He's ______________________.
3. They're happy ______________________.

## 3 Choose, draw, and write.

| Susan | are | an | which | but | interesting | is |
|---|---|---|---|---|---|---|
| She's | bought | car | expensive | climbing | | |

| book. | tomorrow | she | drove | to | it |
|---|---|---|---|---|---|
| brother | Now | they | is | reading | backpack |

| Tuesday | on | the | or | and | or | isn't | TV | getting off |
|---|---|---|---|---|---|---|---|---|
| | | kitchen | bus, | mother | she | doesn't | | |

| fast | her | stop. | or | is | going to | sofa |
|---|---|---|---|---|---|---|
| at | catch | beautiful | She | quiet | | |

| sofa | talk | taxi | because | reading | yesterday. |
|---|---|---|---|---|---|
| take | a | slower | or | she's | late. |

Susan bought an ______________________________

______________________________

______________________________

______________________________.

## 4 Read and sort.

| Alvin's Calendar | | |
|---|---|---|
| Yesterday's Date: *Friday, March 13th* | Today's Date: *Saturday, March 14th* | Tomorrow's Date: *Sunday, March 15th* |
|  |  |  |

1. Yesterday, ____________________________________________.
2. *Today, it's sunny. Alvin is going swimming. He's wearing a swimsuit, and he has a towel*.
3. Tomorrow, ____________________________________________.

## 5 Write, draw, and answer for yourself.

### My Calendar

| Yesterday's Date: ____________ | Today's Date: ____________ | Tomorrow's Date: ____________ |
|---|---|---|
| | | |

1. What did you do yesterday? ____________________________.
2. What are you doing today? ____________________________.
3. What are you going to do tomorrow? ____________________________.

## 1 Listen and write *A* (Angela) or *V* (Vicky). 11

ANGELA: How was your weekend?

VICKY: It was wonderful! On Friday, I went shopping and bought a beautiful dress. On Saturday, I put on my new dress and went dancing. And on Sunday, I went sailing on the lake! How about you?

ANGELA: On Friday, I went swimming, but I caught a cold. So on Saturday and Sunday, I stayed home and slept!

VICKY: I'm sorry! I hope you feel better soon!

V 

## 2 Read the dialogue with a friend.

## 3 Talk with a friend. Then write.

A: How was your last holiday?

B: It was __________. I went __________ and __________.
How about you?

A: I went __________ and __________. It was __________!

## Let's sing!

**1 Listen and complete.** 12

## New York, New York!

On September 21st, I'm going to ___fly___ to New York.
I'm going to __________ alone; I'm sure I'm going to have fun.

Chorus:
New York, New York, it's a wonderful place to be.
That Big Red __________ is going to welcome me.

I'm going to see the sights; I'm going to walk all __________ long.
I'm going to buy __________ postcards; I'm going to send them to you.

I'm going to buy souvenirs; I'm going to go to the __________.
I'm going to take a night tour; I'm never going to go __________.

I'm going to eat __________; I'm going to watch new movies.
I'm going to shop in Soho; I'm going to __________ gifts for you.

**2 Work with a friend. Say the lyrics using the past.**

*On September 21st, I flew to New York...*

# Unit 5

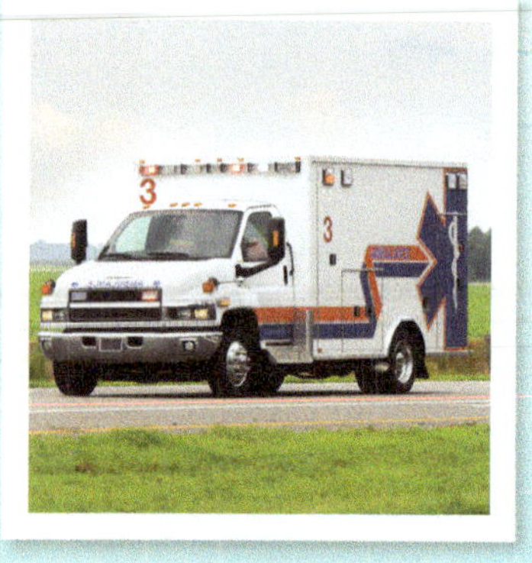
ambulance

cold (*n*)

cough (*v*)

dentist

doctor

(bike) helmet

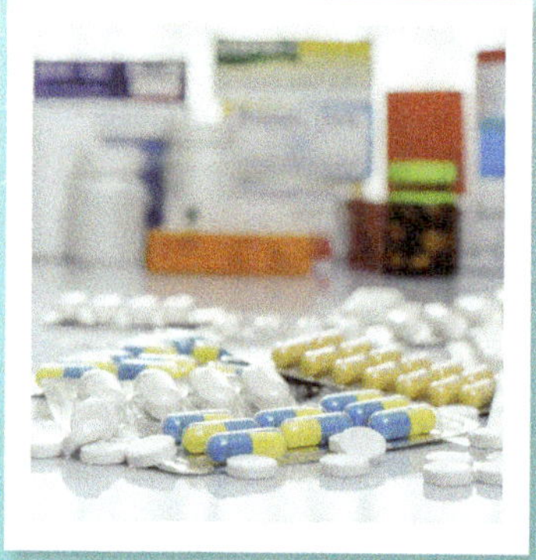
medicine

neck

nurse patient

pie

stomach

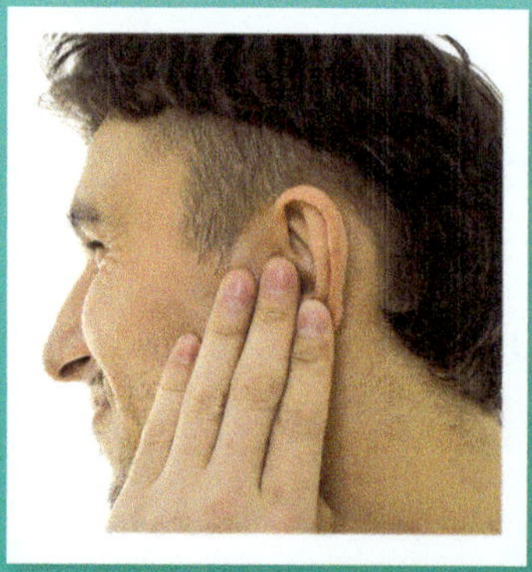
earache

headache

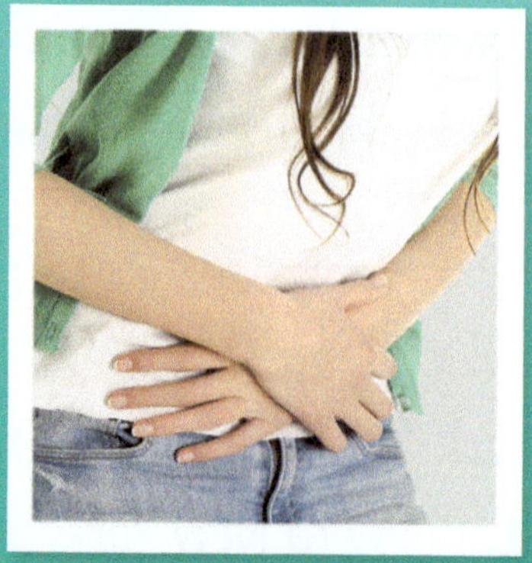
stomachache (*n*)
hurt (*v*)

toothache

# *Should*, affirmative and negative 13

**1 Sort.**

| you should... | When you have a cold, | you shouldn't... |
|---|---|---|
| *call your doctor* | call your doctor | |
| | stay up late | |
| | take medicine | |
| | drink hot tea | |
| | cough on other children | |
| | play outdoors | |

**2 Read and write. Then mark ✓ (*should*) or ✗ (*shouldn't*).**

## Tips for a Healthy Life

1. You *should* listen to your body.
2. You *shouldn't* eat when your stomach feels full.
3. You ________ eat fresh fruits and vegetables.
4. You ________ drink soda.
5. You ________ drink a lot of water.
6. You ________ spend much time playing video games.

☐ 

✓ 

☐ 

☐ 

# Should, interrogative

**Should** I wear a jacket? Yes, you **should**. / No, you **shouldn't**.
What **should** I do? You **should** wear a hat.

## 1 Read, unscramble, and write.

*Linda and Brian had a car accident. Linda hurt her neck. Brian hurt his foot.*

1. Brian / walk around / Should
   *Should Brian walk around*_______? *No, he shouldn't*_______.
2. Linda / neck / move / Should / her
   _______________? _______________.
3. they / Should / ambulance / an / call
   _______________? *Yes,* _______________.

## 2 Read, follow, and write.

| | |
|---|---|
| Henry has a stomachache. | Go to the dentist. |
| Mark and Amy have toothaches. | Stay home and sleep. |
| Mom has a headache. | Eat a little bread and water. |
| I have a terrible cold. | Take medicine. |

1. *What should Henry do*_______? *He should eat a little bread and water*_______.
2. _______________? _______________.
3. _______________? _______________.
4. _______________? _______________.

# Have to, affirmative and negative

I **have to** ride the bus. She **has to** get up early.
I **don't have to** walk to school. She **doesn't have to** make lunch.

## 1 Write and match. Then number.

1. They *have to* study,
2. I ________ get up early,
3. You ________ rest,
4. Mr. Gray ________ run,
5. We ________ take a taxi,

or

I'm going to be late for school.
we're going to get wet.
the train is going to leave without him.
they aren't going to pass the test.
you aren't going to feel better.

## 2 Read and write.

| doesn't have to | don't have to | has to | have to |
|---|---|---|---|

1. The exam isn't easy. I *have to* study hard.
2. It isn't raining. You ________________ take your umbrella.
3. Pam feels fine today. She ________________ go to the doctor.
4. The road is dangerous. Mom ________________ drive carefully.

**Does** he **have to** ride the bus? Yes, he does. / No, he doesn't.
What **does** he **have to** do? He **has to** go to school.

**1 Look, read, and write.**

## Welcome to City Clinic!

Doctor Melinda Ortiz sees patients: 3–4 p.m.
Nurse Jim Adams visits patients: 12–3 p.m.
Receptionist Pat Clark writes down information.

**Clinic Rules**

- Tell the receptionist what hurts.
- Parents: stay next to your children at all times.
- Children: don't run around the waiting room.
- Cover your mouth when you cough.

1. *Do* you *have to* cover your mouth when you cough? *Yes, you do*.
2. ________ children ________ visit patients? ________.
3. ________ the receptionist ________ tell you what hurts? ________.
4. ________ the nurse ________ visit patients in the afternoon? ________.

**2 Look again, read, and answer.**

1. Who has to write down new information? *The receptionist*.
2. What does the nurse have to do? ________.
3. Where do parents have to stay? ________.
4. When does the doctor have to see patients? ________.

## *Had to*, affirmative and negative

**1 Draw and write.**

1 a cough  2 a cold  3 a headache  4 an earache  5 a toothache

go to the doctor

take medicine

drink hot tea

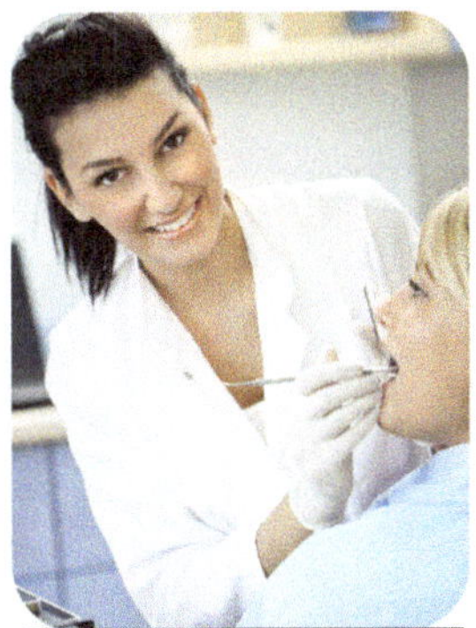
call the dentist

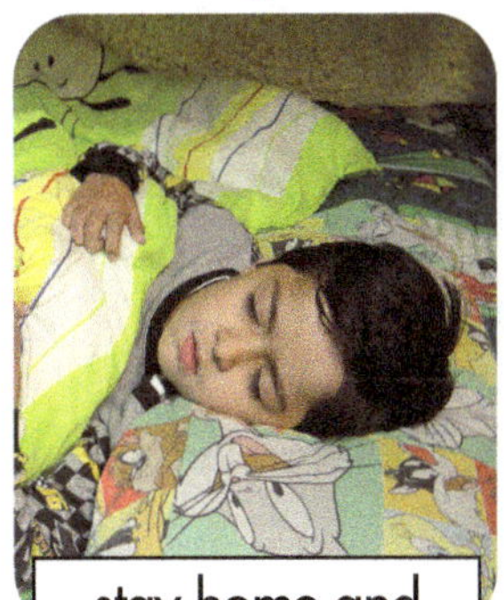
stay home and sleep

1. Yesterday I *had a cough, so I had to drink hot tea*.
2. Last week, my sisters ______________________________,
   so ______________________________.
3. This morning, I ______________________________,
   so ______________________________.
4. Last weekend, Dad ______________________________,
   so ______________________________.
5. Two days ago, my grandmother ______________________________,
   so ______________________________.

**1 Look and mark (✓ or ✗).**

## Park Rules

1

[✗] Stand on the swings.

2

[ ] Fight with other children.

3

[ ] Wear shoes at all times.

4

[ ] Throw your trash in the trash cans.

5

[ ] Run in the street.

6

[ ] Stand in line for the slide.

**2 Now correct the ✗s in your notebook. Use *mustn't*.**

## 3 Read, write, and match.

| had | have | should | don't have | mustn't | shouldn't |
|---|---|---|---|---|---|

*Coach Davis*:

A few years ago, I fell off my bike and hurt my knee.
I __________ to go to the doctor.
Don't be like me. Remember these tips to ride your bike safely!

### Bike Safety

1. You ___should___ always protect your head with a helmet.
2. You ___shouldn't___ ride a bike that is too big or too small.
3. You __________ ride your bike in the middle of the road. It's against the law!
4. Follow traffic rules. You __________ to signal with your hand before turning.
5. You __________ to stop at stop signs and red lights, too.
6. You __________ to wear fluorescent bands so people can see you. But it's a good idea!
7. You __________ wear headphones when riding your bike.
8. You __________ check your bike before riding it. All smart bikers do!

## 1 Listen and write. 14

JAMES: Hello, nurse. You *have to* ________ help me.

NURSE: What's the matter?

JAMES: I ________ a terrible ________!

NURSE: Why?

JAMES: Because I entered a pie-eating contest, and I won!

NURSE: Oh, dear. You ________ eat a lot of pie all at once.

JAMES: I ________ eat a lot to win! But now my ________ really hurts.

NURSE: You ________ take this medicine to help your ________.
But you ________ eat so much pie again!

JAMES: I know now! Thanks, nurse.

## 2 Read the dialogue with a friend.

## 3 Talk with a friend. Then write.

| stomachache | toothache |
|---|---|

| arm | head | leg |
|---|---|---|

A: What's the matter?

B: My ________ hurts. / I have a ________.

A: Why?

B: Because ________________________.

A: You should ________________________.

## Let's sing!

1 **Read and circle. Then listen and check.** 15

### We Have to, We Should

Chorus:
We have to, we have to, we have to do
Everything our teachers tell us to.
We have to, we have to, we have to do
Everything our parents tell us to.

You ***should*** / ***shouldn't***  go to school.

You ***should*** / ***shouldn't*** learn the  rule.

You ***should*** / ***shouldn't*** jump in the  pool.
You ***should*** / ***shouldn't*** be a fool!

You ***should*** / ***shouldn't*** help at home.
You ***should*** / ***shouldn't*** use the 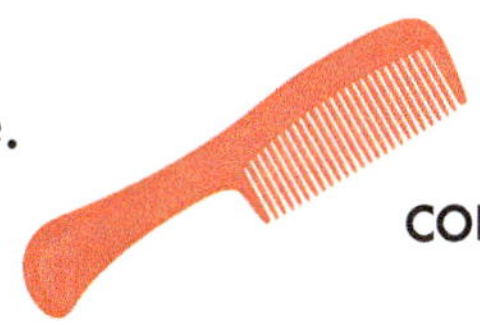 comb.
You ***should*** / ***shouldn't*** stay alone.

You ***should*** / ***shouldn't*** talk on the  phone!

You ***should*** / ***shouldn't*** never be mean.
You ***should*** / ***shouldn't*** eat your green  beans.
You ***should*** / ***shouldn't*** leave your team.

You ***should*** / ***shouldn't*** yell or  scream!

# Unit 6

feather

field

island

jungle

1 leaf, 2 leaves

moon stars

mountain

plant (*n*)

plant (*v*)

pollution

road

rocket

scare (*v*)

weather forecast

world

# Possessive forms, 's, s'

## 1 Color, read, and write.

1. *Dad / jacket*
   Dad's jacket is red.
2. *the girls / swimsuits*
   ______.
3. *Mom / hat*
   ______.
4. *Grandpa / shorts*
   ______.
5. *the plants / leaves*
   ______.
6. *Grandma / dress*
   ______.
7. *the birds / feathers*
   ______.
8. *Dad / shoes*
   ______.

# Simple future, affirmative

I will → I'll you will → you'll we will → we'll
he / she / it will → he'll / she'll / it'll they will → they'll

**1 Look and write.**

be discover take travel watch

## My Dream Life in the Future

1. When I grow up, (*I*) *I'll be* ______ the best scientist in the world.
2. (*I*) ____________ all over the world with other scientists.
3. (*We*) ____________ birds in the fields and mountains.
4. (*We*) ____________ a new kind of plant in the jungle.
5. (*I*) ____________ some leaves home with me.
6. (*They*) ____________ in my museum for everyone to see.

# Simple future, negative

**1 Read and circle true (*T*) or false (*F*).**

One hundred years from now, things will be very different in our cities. Today, cars and planes use gasoline that causes pollution. But in the future, there will be electric flying cars. The air will be clean. People will be healthy.

People will also have more time to have fun instead of working hard at home. There will be special robots that help people. The robots will cook, clean the house, and go to the grocery store!

1. A hundred years from now, our cities will be the same. T (F)
2. There will be flying cars instead of airplanes. T F
3. Cars will need gasoline. T F
4. People will get sick from pollution. T F
5. People will work harder than they do today. T F

**2 Rewrite the false statements. Use *won't*.**

*A hundred years from now, our cities won't be the same.*

______________________________

______________________________

______________________________

# Simple future, interrogative 16

## 1 Look, unscramble, and write.

**Next Week in Our Town**

| Monday | Tuesday | Wednesday | Thursday | Friday |
|---|---|---|---|---|
| Restaurants closed: eat at home | Farmer's market: fresh fruit | Annual book sale at the library | Mayor's Town Hall speech | Family festival in the park |
|  |  |  |  |  |



1. be / closed / will / the restaurants / on Monday
   *Will the restaurants be closed on Monday* ? *Yes, they will* .
2. will / fruit / the farmers / on Tuesday / sell
   ______________________________ ? __________ .
3. at the town hall / on Wednesday / speak / the mayor / will
   ______________________________ ? __________ .
4. have / a book sale / will / the library / on Thursday
   ______________________________ ? __________ .
5. to the park / families / go / on Friday / will
   ______________________________ ? __________ .

# Who will...?

**1 Draw and write.**

*Tomorrow is the town's clean-up day. There will be a lot of work to do!*

1. pick up trash
2. cut down the old plants
3. clean leaves from the roads
4. paint the school
5. plant new flowers

Charlie

Paul

Lily and Vicky

Daisy

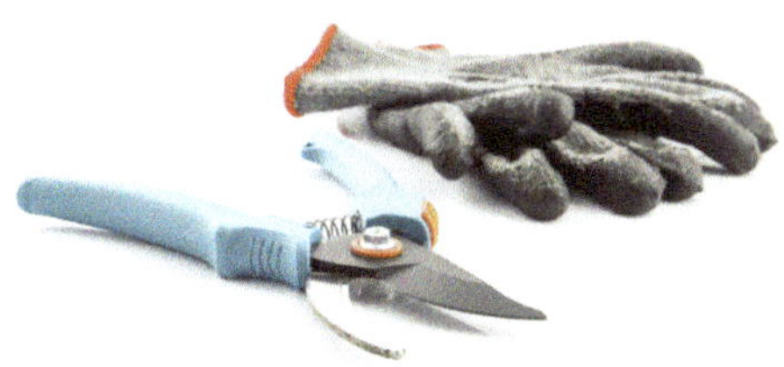

Peter

1. Who will pick up trash ? Charlie .
2. Who ______ ? ______ .
3. ______ ? ______ .
4. ______ ? ______ .
5. ______ ? ______ .

## *Will*, other question words

**1 Read the answers and write the questions. Match.**

eat go to school live study travel wear

___ 150 years.

___ On Earth and on the moon.

___ Dried fruit and vegetables.

_1_ Special plastic clothes.

___ Flying and astronomy (the study of the stars)

___ By rocket.

1. What *will people wear* ________?
2. How ________?
3. Where ________?
4. Which subjects ________?
5. What ________?
6. How long ________?

**2 Write and draw your prediction for the future.**

I think that in the future, ________.

## 3 Look and write.

1. It will be rainy and cool in London ___.
2. ___.
3. ___.
4. ___.
5. ___.

## 4 Read and answer for yourself.

### It's time to make your resolutions!

A *resolution* is something you will do or won't do. People make resolutions because they want to live healthier, better lives in the next year.

**What are your resolutions for next year?**

1. I won't ride my bike without a helmet ___.
2. I will ___.
3. ___.
4. ___.
5. ___.

Let's talk!

## 1 Listen and write. 17

MARY: *Where will* we go for the holidays?

MOM: We'll go to Grandma's house at the __________.

MARY: Wow! __________ we do there?

MOM: We'll __________ and lie on the __________.

MARY: __________ we wear?

MOM: It'll be hot, so we'll wear __________________!

MARY: That will be fun. Here, everyone will be wearing __________________!

## 2 Read the dialogue with a friend.

## 3 Talk with a friend. Then write.

an island

the jungle

the mountains

the city

A: Someday, I'll go on my dream vacation!

B: Where will you go?

A: I'll go to ______________.

B: Who will go with you?

A: ______________ will go with me.

B: What will you do there?

A: We'll ______________.

B: It sounds wonderful!

## Let's sing!

**1 Listen, underline, and sort.** 18

### I'll Try to Be Me

Sometimes I wonder what I will do
When I grow up. Don't you?
Will I be rich, will I be poor?
Will I be a famous rock star for sure?
Where will I travel?
What will I say?
Who will I date?
How much will I weigh?

Sometimes I wonder where I will be
When I grow up. You see?
Will I be short, will I be tall?
Will I be working in a shopping mall?
Where will I live?
What will I wear?
Who will I have fun with?
How much will I care?

Sometimes I wonder where I will go
When I grow up. You know?
Will I be ugly, will I be cheap?
Will I drive around the world in a jeep?
I don't really know
How my life will be,
But I'll try to be happy
I'll try to be me!

| Adjectives | Verbs |
|---|---|
| rich | wonder |
| poor | do |
| | be |
| | grow |

# Unit 7

airport

basement

blanket

crumbs

film (*v*)

moustache

movie star, star

oven

pilot

police officer

shop (*v*)

shower

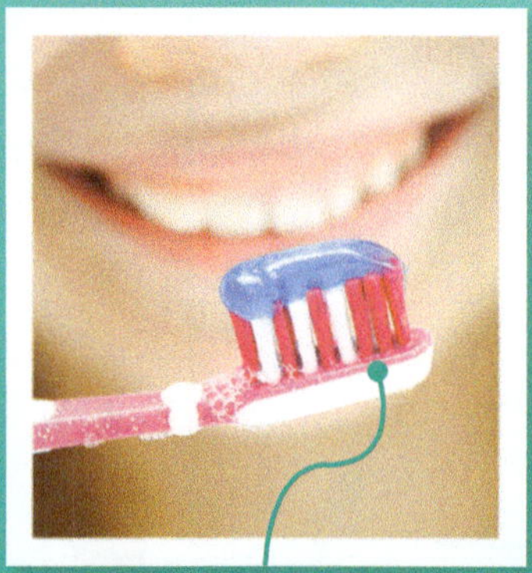
toothbrush

upstairs (*adv*)

downstairs (*adv*)

work (*n*, *v*)

# Sequencing words

**1 Look, number, and write.**

*First, Daniel climbed a tree. Next, a branch* ____________________

________________________________________

________________________________________

*First, the pilot gets dressed.* ____________________

________________________________________

________________________________________

## 2 Trace, match, and write.

First | Finally | Next | Then

eat cookies | fall asleep | go downstairs | play with toys

basement | bedroom | living room | kitchen

*First, the boy went downstairs to the basement.* ______________________

______________________________________________

______________________________________________.

## 3 Write about yourself.

What do you do every morning?

First, I ______________________. Next, I ______________________.

Then, I ______________________. Finally, I ______________________.

## Relative pronoun, *where* 19

**1 Look and write. Use *where*.**

**Take a Trip to the Movies on the Hollywood Bus!**

**Grauman's Chinese Theater**
Learn about Hollywood's history at this first bus stop!

**Movie Studios**
Watch people filming movies in these places!

**Beverly Hills**
See movie stars' homes in this famous city!

**Rodeo Drive**
Shop like movie stars on this expensive street!

**Griffith Observatory**
See *real* stars (in the night sky) at this science center!

1. (*bus stop*) *It's the bus stop where you can learn about Hollywood's history* ____.
2. (*places*) *They're the places where* ____.
3. (*houses*) ____.
4. (*stores*) ____.
5. (*stars*) ____.

# Relative pronoun, *who*

## 1 Follow and write. Use *who*.

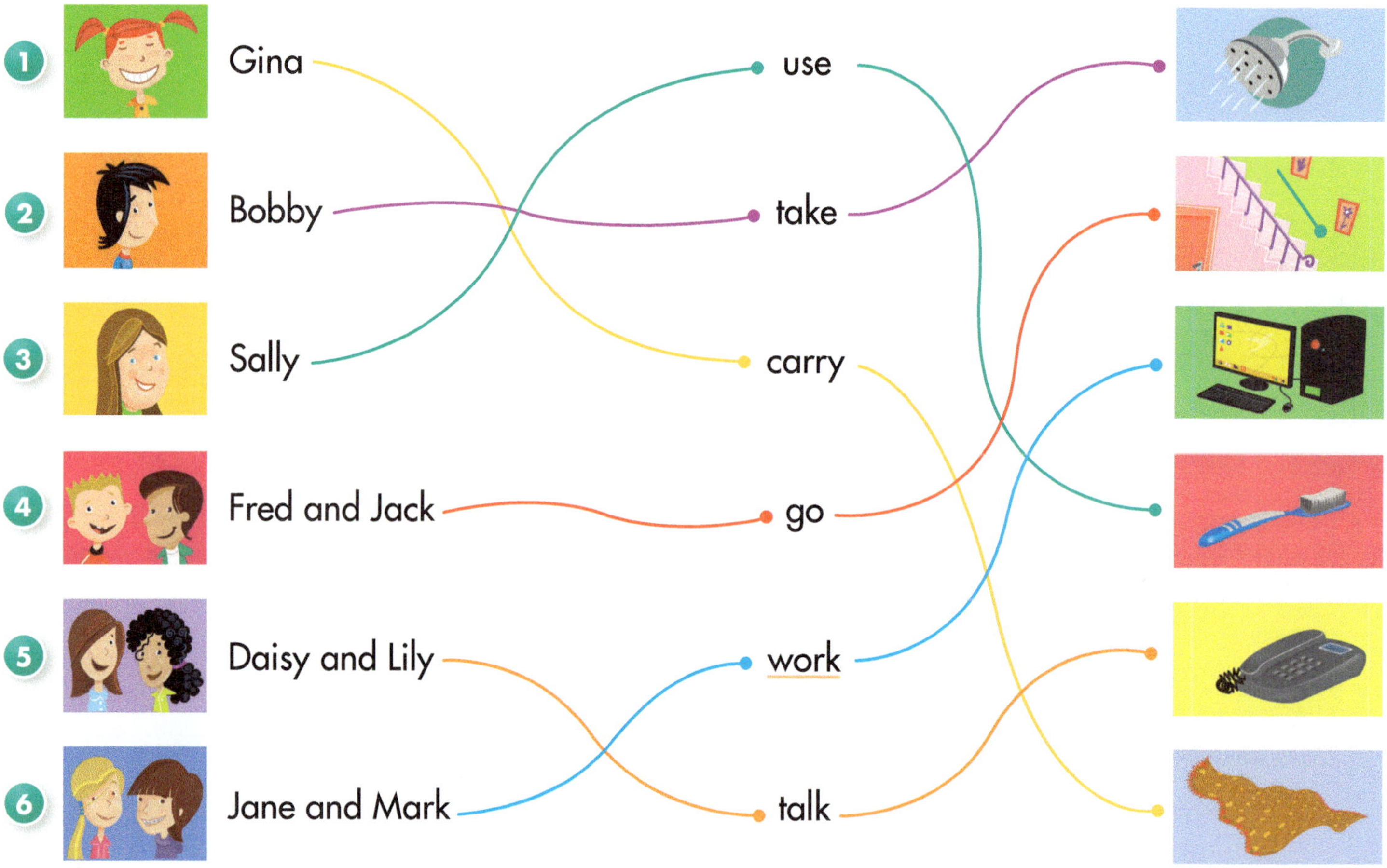


1. Gina is the girl who is carrying a blanket ______.
2. Bobby is the boy who is ______.
3. ______.
4. ______.
5. ______.
6. ______.

# Relative pronoun, *that*

**1 Look, number, and write. Use *that*.**

| be | chase | eat | fall | find | have |
|---|---|---|---|---|---|

1

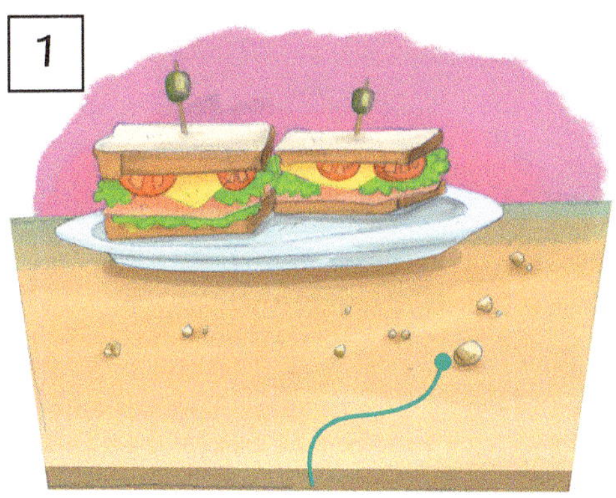

1. These are the crumbs *that were* ______ on the table.
2. This is the mouse ______ the crumbs.
3. This is the cat *that chased* ______ the mouse.
4. These are the sandwiches ______ off the table.
5. This is the dog ______ the sandwiches.
6. This is the boy ______ didn't ______ lunch!

## 2 Look and write.

that where who

catch drive help work

1. Police officers: people *who catch criminals* __________
2. Police car: a car ______________________________
3. Police station: a place __________________________
4. Police dogs: animals ___________________________

that where who

catch hit play throw

5. Pitcher: the person *who throws the baseball* __________
6. Baseball diamond: the place ______________________
7. Catcher: the person _____________________________
8. Bat: the thing _________________________________

## 3 Circle and write about yourself.

1. I like people ***who*** / ***where*** __________________________.
2. I like places ***who*** / ***where*** __________________________.

**4** **Read, circle, and write.**

First Finally Next Then

### How to Clean Your Room—Fast!

__________, pick up your toys and clothes.
You ***should*** / ***shouldn't*** throw them on the floor!
__________, make your bed. You ***should*** / ***shouldn't*** make your bed every day!
__________, clean desks, tables, and windows.
You ***should*** / ***shouldn't*** use glass cleaner for windows.
__________, enjoy your nice, clean room.
You ***should*** / ***shouldn't*** let it get so messy again!

**5** **Read, write, and draw.**

I had a terrible day. Everything went wrong! Here's what happened...

First, ______________________________.

__________, ______________________________.

__________, ______________________________.

__________, ______________________________.

Let's talk!

**1 Listen and circle.** 20

BILL: Let's plan our day. What should we do?

JILL: Let's do / ***make*** our homework first. Then we won't ***do*** / ***make*** mistakes because we're in a hurry.

BILL: Okay. Next, let's ***do*** / ***make*** the chores. But we don't have to ***do*** / ***make*** the bed because I already did.

JILL: Thanks! Then, let's eat lunch. I'll ***do*** / ***make*** our food...

BILL: And I'll ***do*** / ***make*** the dishes afterward.

JILL: Great! Finally, let's ***do*** / ***make*** something fun.

BILL: Okay. We can ***do*** / ***make*** a craft or ***do*** / ***make*** a puzzle!

**Bill and Jill's Plan**

10 a.m.

11 a.m.

1 p.m.

2 p.m.

**2 Read the dialogue with a friend.**

**3 Talk with a friend. Then write.**

| ***do...*** | | ***make...*** | | |
|---|---|---|---|---|
| the chores | exercise | breakfast | crafts | a mess |
| laundry | homework | lunch | friends | your bed |
| the dishes | a puzzle | dinner | | |

A: Let's make a plan. What should we do today?

B: First, let's do _______________.

A: Great! Next, let's make _______________.

B: Then, let's make _______________.

A: Okay. Finally, let's do _______________.

B: Let's get started!

## Let's sing!

**1 Listen, read, and write.** 21

First Next Then

like milk put sing

### Instructions

Chorus:
Instructions here,
Instructions there.
I see instructions everywhere.

___First___, plug the toaster in.
_________, _________ the bread inside.
_________, watch those slices burn.
They said it worked. They lied!

_________, pour some _________ in the blender.
_________, add some sugar, a lot.
_________, turn the speed to *high*.
Oops, I forgot the top!

_________, put the batteries in.
_________, turn the radio on.
_________, find the station you _________.
Come on, _________ your favorite song!

# Unit 8

CD player (*n*)

chop (*v*)

elevator (*n*)

peel (*v*)

roof (*n*)

salad dressing, dressing (*n*)

seat (*n*)

stretch (*v*)

spread (*v*)

above (*prep*) below (*prep*)

around (*prep*)

inside (*prep*) outside (*prep*)

into (*prep*) out of (*prep*)

## Commands, affirmative

**1 Look and match.**

☐

1

☐

☐

☐

☐

☐

☐

☐

1. Open the windows.
2. Wash your hands!
3. Put on your raincoat.
4. Hurry up!
5. Look at the board.
6. Climb up quickly!
7. Be quiet.
8. Answer the phone.
9. Get off the sofa!

# Commands, negative

**1 Read, number, and write.**

| | |
|---|---|
| 1. Jump. | *Don't jump*__________________, please. |
| 2. Touch the dog. | ____________________________. |
| 3. Eat the cake. | Dad, ____________________________! |
| 4. Now go to sleep, Bobby. | ____________________________ at work. |
| 5. Feed the animals. | ____________________________. |

# Ask, *want* someone to do something 22

## 1 Look and match.

1. *Mom*: Jake, please wash the lettuce.
2. *Jake*: Dad, please chop the tomatoes.
3. *Dad*: Amy, please peel the carrots.
4. *Mom*: Jake and Amy, please mix the dressing.
5. *Amy*: Mom and Dad, please put the salad in bowls.
6. *Mom*: Please eat your salad, Amy, Jake, and Dad!

1. (*ask*) *Mom asked Jake to wash the lettuce* ________.
2. (*want*) ________________________________________.
3. (*ask*) ________________________________________.
4. (*want*) ________________________________________.
5. (*ask*) ________________________________________.
6. (*want*) ________________________________________.

# Prepositions of location

**1 Look and write.**

1

2

3

4

8

7

6

5

1. Climb ***in*** / ***up*** the ramp.
2. Walk ***above*** / ***down*** the ramp.
3. Go ***into*** / ***over*** the tunnel.
4. Come ***off*** / ***out of*** the tunnel.
5. Jump ***under*** / ***off*** the ramp.
6. Run ***around*** / ***over*** the poles.
7. Run ***above*** / ***around*** the ground.
8. Jump ***over*** / ***up*** the bar.

## 2 Write and number.

above around down in inside into off out of outside up

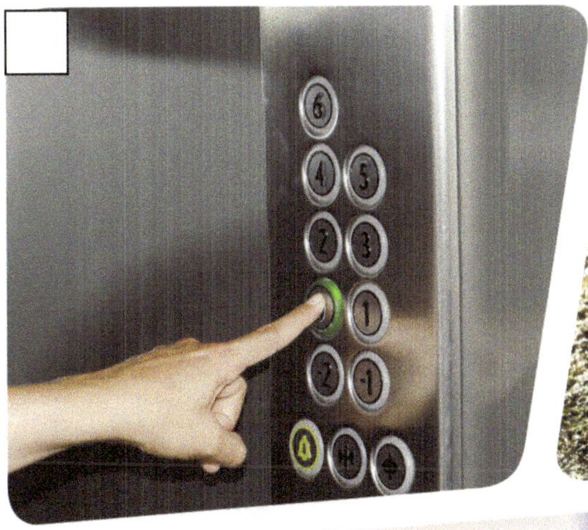

1

1. Don't ever jump off_____ a roof! Climb down_____ the ladder carefully.
2. Sit i_____ your seat. Don't run a_____ the classroom.
3. Are your shoes dirty? Stay o_____ the house. Don't go i_____!
4. Please take the wet towels o_____ o_____ the washing machine and put them i_____ the dryer.
5. The doctor's office is a_____ the store. Take the elevator u_____ one floor.

## 3 Unscramble and write.

1. Stretch your legs _________ (*b e r o e f*) a race.
2. Put one leg in front of you and lean forward, with your head _________ (*a v b e o*) your knee.
3. _________ (*a r e t f*) thirty seconds, switch to the other leg.

## 4 Look and write.

Finally First Next Then

around below into off on out of to

1. ___First___, cut a circle __________ foam or construction paper.
2. __________, use a pen or pencil to draw a face __________ it.
3. __________, wind the green pipe cleaner __________ your index finger.
4. __________, take the puppet __________ your finger and attach the head.
5. __________, cut the black pipe cleaner __________ two pieces.
6. __________, attach the black pipe cleaners __________ the body to make the legs.

## 5 Look again and label the steps.

### How to Make a Fun Finger Puppet

______first______

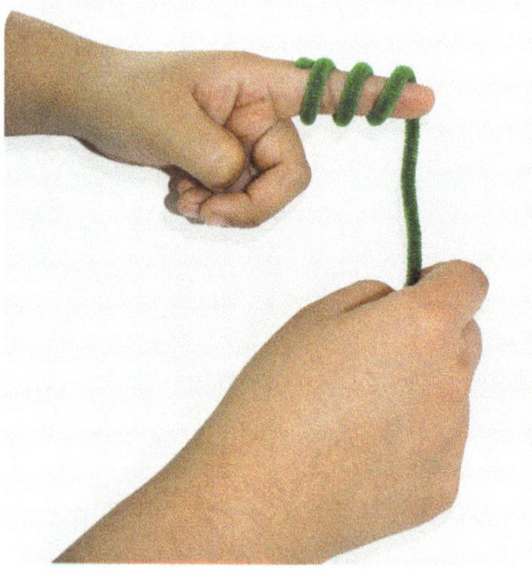

__________________

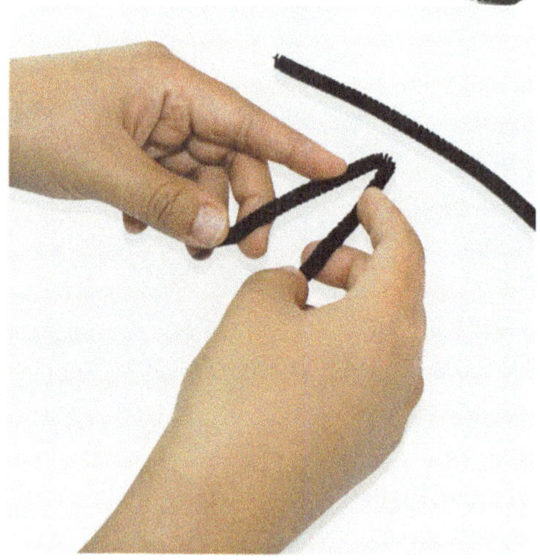

__________________

__________________

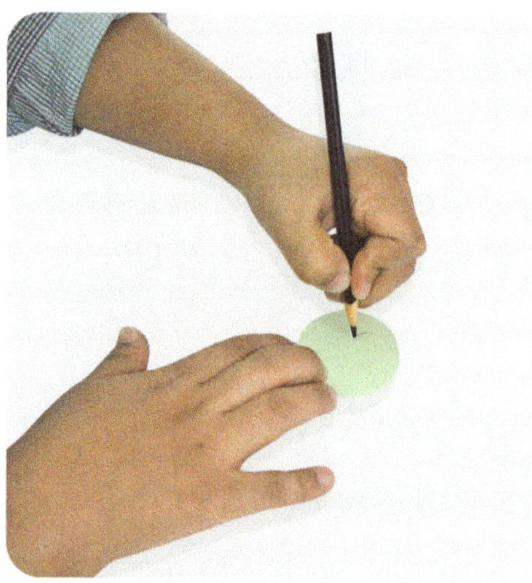

__________________

______sixth______

## 6 Look, number, and write.

| add | put | roll up | spread | take |
|---|---|---|---|---|

| inside | into | on | on top of | out of |
|---|---|---|---|---|

### How to Make a Pizza Wrap

☐ 1 ☐ ☐

1. First, ___spread___ pizza sauce ___on___ a flour tortilla.
2. Next, __________ cheese and vegetables __________ the pizza sauce.
3. Then, __________ the tortilla with the cheese and vegetables __________ it.
4. Finally, __________ the tortilla __________ the microwave.
5. After two minutes, __________ the tortilla __________ the microwave. Enjoy!

## 7 Write and draw about yourself.

Yesterday, __________ asked me to ______________________________.

Let's talk!

## 1 Listen and write. 23

again back carefully first much never on really

JILL: I ___really___ like our new TV, Mom!
MOM: Me, too! Let's watch something. Please turn it ________.
JILL: Nothing's happening. Should I shake it?
MOM: No, ________ shake a TV.
JILL: Should we take it ________ to the store?
MOM: Hmm... Let's read the instructions ________.
JILL: Okay. Here they are. "________, plug it in."
MOM: Oh! I forgot! There. Try it ________.
JILL: Great! It's working ________ better now!

## 2 Read the dialogue with a friend.

## 3 Talk with a friend. Then write.

carefully down in on up

A: How do we use our new CD player correctly?
B: Let's look at the instructions.
A: First, ________________.
B: Second, ________________.
A: Third, ________________.
B: Fourth, ________________.
A: Fifth, *adjust the volume*________________.

## Let's sing!

**1 Listen, read, and write.** 24

| from | over | to | up | with |
|---|---|---|---|---|

### Up and Far Away

Look ________ at the big black sky.
Come ________ me and we can fly.
We can see Earth from far away;
See the change ________ night
________ day.
An astronaut says: "See you soon!
My space ship is ready to go
________ the moon."

Planet Jupiter is big and old,
And Mars is red and cold.
Satellites travel all ________
the place,
And bring us news ________
outer space.

# Grammar summary

Unit 1

**How often...?**

| | | | | |
|---|---|---|---|---|
| How often | do | I / you | feed the rabbit? | Once a month. |
| | does | he / she / it | drink water? | Twice a day. |
| | do | we / you / they | walk the dog? | Three times a week. |
| | | | eat vegetables? | Every day. |
| | | | | Never. |

**Adverbs of manner**

The baby is crying **loudly**.
The boys are behaving **badly**.
People talk **quietly** in a library.

The man is **slowly** walking downstairs.
They are **happily** opening the presents.
Jessie **sadly** shakes her head.

Unit 2

***As ... as* for the same**

The lion is **as big as** the tiger.
Lions are **as big as** tigers.

The cat isn't **as big as** the tiger.
Cats aren't **as big as** tigers.

**Comparative and superlative adjectives, *-er, -est***

Monday

65°F / 18°C

Tuesday

60°F / 15°C

Wednesday

55°F / 13°C

*cold:* Tuesday was **colder than** Monday. Wednesday was **the coldest** of all.
*wet:* Tuesday was **wetter than** Monday. Wednesday was **the wettest** of all.
*rainy:* Tuesday was **rainier than** Monday. Wednesday was **the rainiest** of all.

## Comparative and superlative adjectives, *more, most*

*comfortable*: The sofa was **more comfortable than** the chair.
The bed was **the most comfortable** of all.

## Comparative and superlative adjectives, *good, bad*

*good*: Basketball is **better than** baseball. Soccer is **the best** sport of all.
*bad*: Rainy days are **worse than** cloudy days. Snowy days are **the worst** of all.

## *There was, There were*

Unit 3

| Uncountable nouns | Countable nouns |
|---|---|
| There was cheese in the fridge.<br>There wasn't any milk.<br>Was there any chocolate?<br>Yes, there was. / No, there wasn't. | There were TVs in 1923.<br>There weren't any DVD players.<br>Were there any computers?<br>Yes, there were. / No, there weren't. |

## *How much...? How many...?*

| Uncountable nouns | Countable nouns |
|---|---|
| **How much** popcorn was there in the bag?<br>There was some / a little / a lot of popcorn.<br>There wasn't any popcorn. | **How many** cookies were there in the box?<br>There were three cookies.<br>There weren't any cookies. |

## *Use to*, affirmative and negative

| | | |
|---|---|---|
| I / You<br>He / She / It<br>We / You / They | used to<br>didn't use to | jump in the air.<br>run fast.<br>use the Internet.<br>ride horses. |

## *Use to*, interrogative

| | | | | |
|---|---|---|---|---|
| Did | I<br>you | use to | eat tomatoes?<br>go camping?<br>swim in the river?<br>study hard? | Yes, you did. / No, you didn't.<br>Yes, I did. / No, I didn't. |
| | he / she / it | | | Yes, he / she / it did.<br>No, he / she / it didn't. |
| | we / you / they | | | Yes, you / we / they did.<br>No, you / we / they didn't. |

## *Be*, simple past, affirmative

| | | |
|---|---|---|
| I | was | happy.<br>sad.<br>in the United States. |
| You | were | |
| He / She / It | was | |
| We / You / They | were | |

Unit 4

## *Be*, simple past, negative

| | | | |
|---|---|---|---|
| I | was not | (wasn't) | sad.<br>on the bus.<br>in the kitchen. |
| You | were not | (weren't) | |
| He / She / It | was not | (wasn't) | |
| We / You / They | were not | (weren't) | |

## *Be*, past simple, interrogative

| | | | |
|---|---|---|---|
| Was | I | funny?<br>interesting?<br>in the house? | Yes, you were. / No, you weren't. |
| Were | you | | Yes, I was. / No, I wasn't. |
| Was | he / she / it | | Yes, he /she / it was.<br>No, he / she / it wasn't. |
| Were | we / you / they | | Yes, you / we / they were.<br>No, you / we / they weren't. |

| Simple past of regular verbs, affirmative | |
|---|---|
| I<br>You<br>He / She / It<br>We / You / They | play**ed** in the snow.<br>travel**ed** to Italy.<br>walk**ed** around the school.<br>wash**ed** the towels. |

| Irregular verbs in past | | | | | | | |
|---|---|---|---|---|---|---|---|
| buy | bought | eat | ate | hurt | hurt | wake up | woke up |
| drink | drank | fall | fell | make | made | wear | wore |
| drive | drove | go | went | put on | put on | | |
| dry | dried | have | had | take | took | | |

| Simple past, negative | | |
|---|---|---|
| I<br>You<br>He / She / It<br>We / You / They | did not<br>(didn't) | watch TV.<br>make a sandwich.<br>go fishing.<br>put on a coat. |

| Simple past, interrogative | | | |
|---|---|---|---|
| Did | I | take a taxi?<br>buy a sweater?<br>wear a uniform?<br>cheer? | Yes, you did. / No, you didn't. |
| | you | | Yes, I did. / No, I didn't. |
| | he / she / it | | Yes, he / she / it did.<br>No, he / she / it didn't. |
| | we / you / they | | Yes, you / we / they did.<br>No, you / we / they didn't. |

| Conjunctions |
|---|
| I like chocolate ice cream **and** vanilla ice cream. |
| Would you like a hamburger **or** a hot dog? |
| You washed the clothes, **but** you didn't dry them! |
| They're happy **because** they bought a car. |

| *Should*, affirmative and negative | | |
|---|---|---|
| I | should<br>should not<br>(shouldn't) | call the doctor.<br>take medicine.<br>ride your bike too fast.<br>call an ambulance. |
| You | | |
| He / She / It | | |
| We / You / They | | |

| *Should*, interrogative | | | |
|---|---|---|---|
| Should | I | eat vegetables?<br>stay up late?<br>play outdoors?<br>drink hot tea? | Yes, you should. / No, you shouldn't. |
| | you | | Yes, I should. / No, I shouldn't. |
| | he / she / it | | Yes, he / she / it should.<br>No, he / she / it shouldn't. |
| | we / you / they | | Yes, you / we / they should.<br>No, you / we / they shouldn't. |

| *What should I do?* | | | | | | |
|---|---|---|---|---|---|---|
| What | should | I<br>you | do? | You<br>I | should | wear a suit.<br>walk.<br>call the hospital.<br>eat a little bread. |
| | | he / she / it | | He / She / It | | |
| | | we / you / they | | You / We / They | | |

| *Have to*, affirmative | | |
|---|---|---|
| I | have to | study.<br>take a taxi.<br>get up early.<br>walk to school. |
| You | | |
| He / She / It | | |
| We / You / They | | |

| *Have to*, negative | | | |
|---|---|---|---|
| I<br>You | don't | have to | read that book.<br>take an umbrella.<br>go to the doctor.<br>eat a lot of food. |
| He / She / It | doesn't | | |
| We / You / They | don't | | |

| *Have to*, interrogative | | | | |
|---|---|---|---|---|
| Do | I | have to | go now?<br>see patients?<br>see the doctor?<br>cook dinner? | Yes, you do. / No, you don't. |
| | you | | | Yes, I do. / No, I don't. |
| Does | he / she / it | | | Yes, he / she / it does.<br>No, he / she / it doesn't. |
| Do | we / you / they | | | Yes, you / we / they do.<br>No, you / we / they don't. |

| *Had to*, affirmative and negative | | |
|---|---|---|
| I | had to<br>didn't have to | take medicine.<br>run in the morning.<br>stand in line.<br>wear a helmet. |
| You | | |
| He / She / It | | |
| We / You / They | | |

| *Mustn't*, prohibition | |
|---|---|
| You mustn't | run in the street.<br>cough on others.<br>throw trash on the ground.<br>be late. |

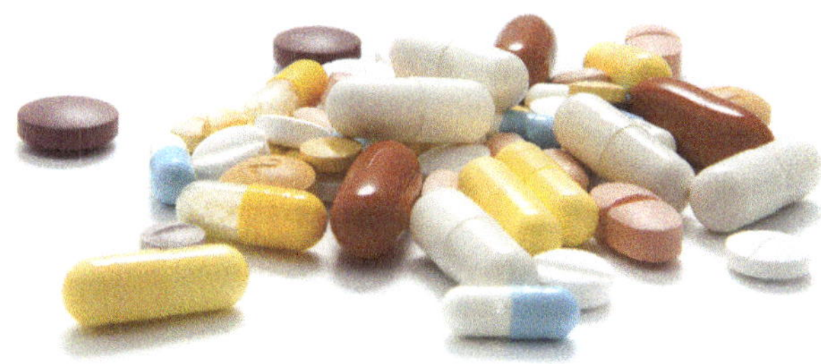

Unit 6

| Possessive forms, *'s, s'* | | |
|---|---|---|
| **Singular nouns** | **Irregular plural nouns** | **Regular plural nouns** |
| Jane's book<br>my aunt's shoes | the children's playground<br>the men's sweaters | my cousins' house<br>the birds' feathers |

| Simple future, affirmative | | | |
|---|---|---|---|
| I | will | (I'll) | fly to France tomorrow.<br>study at home.<br>travel in space.<br>be a scientist in twenty years. |
| You | | (You'll) | |
| He<br>She<br>It | | (He'll)<br>(She'll)<br>(It'll) | |
| We<br>You<br>They | | (We'll)<br>(You'll)<br>(They'll) | |

| Simple future, negative | | |
|---|---|---|
| I<br>You<br>He / She / It<br>We / You / They | won't | drive cars in the future.<br>get sick from pollution.<br>work hard.<br>cook or clean. |

| Simple future, interrogative | | | |
|---|---|---|---|
| Will | I | drive flying cars?<br>use electric power?<br>wear different clothes?<br>go to the beach? | Yes, you will. / No, you won't. |
| | you | | Yes, I will. / No, I won't. |
| | he / she / it | | Yes, he /she / it will.<br>No, he / she / it won't. |
| | we / you / they | | Yes, you / we / they will.<br>No, you /we / they won't. |

| Simple future, question words | |
|---|---|
| **Who** will pick up the trash? | I will! |
| **What** will people wear? | Suits and dresses. |
| **When** will the package arrive? | On Tuesday. |
| **Where** will people live in the future? | On the moon. |
| **Why** will people work less? | Because they will have robots. |
| **How** will people travel in the future? | By rocket. |
| **How long** will a trip around the world take? | Seven days. |

| Sequencing words | | | | | | |
|---|---|---|---|---|---|---|
| First | → | Next | → | Then | → | Finally |

Unit 7

Unit 8

| Relative pronouns, *where, who, that* | | |
|---|---|---|
| where | places | This is the place **where** people film movies. |
| who | people | Anna is the girl **who** is wearing a red shirt. |
| that | people, places, or things | I met the man **that** coached the soccer team.<br>This is the airport **that** is closest to my house.<br>Those are the cookies **that** were in the oven. |

| Commands | |
|---|---|
| **affirmative** | **negative** |
| Open the window. | Don't jump on the bed. |
| Please hurry up! | Please don't feed the animals. |
| Be quiet, please. | Don't sleep! |
| Answer the phone. | Don't eat the cake, please. |

| *Ask, want* someone to do something |
|---|
| Dad **asked** Jason to chop the tomatoes. |
| Mom **wanted** me to peel the carrots. |

| Prepositions of location | | | |
|---|---|---|---|
| above | around | below | down |
| in | inside | into | off |
| out of | outside | over | up |

# Audio script

## Unit 1

**Track 1**

MODERATOR: Okay, are you ready to play? Check your buzzers!
MODERATOR: Listen CAREFULLY! Question one: What color…
BOY: Green!
MODERATOR: No. What color is…
GIRL: Blue!
MODERATOR: No, no. You make mistakes because you answer too QUICKLY! Listen. What color is an elephant?
GIRL: Gray!
MODERATOR: Correct!

**Track 2**

ADAM: Let's put on a show! We can work together. Emily, what are you good at?
EMILY: I'm good at painting pictures.
TIM: Yes, Emily paints very well! She can make the set.
ADAM: That's great! Tim, what are you good at?
TIM: I'm good at talking loudly. I can be an actor!
ADAM: I talk quietly, but I'm good at working carefully. I can do the sound and lights!
EMILY: How about our other friends? What are they good at?
ADAM: They're good at clapping happily. They can be the audience!

**Track 3**
**The Dream Team**
(See page 13.)

## Unit 2

**Track 4**

BEN: Look, Matt! I'm as tall as you!
MATT: That's great, Ben.
BEN: Look, Matt! I'm as strong as you! Oops.
MATT: Ben, please go away.
BEN: Look, Matt! I'm as loud as you!
MATT: Well, I'm not as annoying as you!

**Track 5**

MOM: I think the city is the best place for a vacation!
DAD: Really? I know cities have interesting restaurants and museums, but they're the most expensive!
MOM: That's true. I know the beach is less expensive than the city, and I think it's more beautiful.
JANE: But I think the beach isn't as comfortable as the city. It's the hottest place of all on a sunny day!
DAD: I think a vacation at home is the best. It's less expensive than the beach or the city. We all know it's the most comfortable place to be!

**Track 6**
**Amazing Things**
Chorus:
The most interesting thing on the land,
The most amazing thing in the air,
The most beautiful thing in the sea,
Come and learn about them with me!

England is wet,
Brazil is wetter,
But India is the wettest place of all.

Cancun is hot,
Panama is hotter,
But Libya is the hottest place of all.

(Chorus)

The sea horse is slow,
The turtle is slower,
But the snail is the slowest creature of all.

Cobras are long,
Boas are longer,
But anacondas are the longest snakes of all.

(Chorus)

## Unit 3

### Track 7

BOY: Uh oh. Oh, no. Eeek! Help!
DAD: Wow. I'll help you clean up. How many bags of popcorn were there?
BOY: There was only one bag! Just like you always make!
DAD: Hmm… Okay, but HOW MUCH popcorn was there in the bag? This bag is really big!
BOY: I guess there was A LOT of popcorn. Sorry, Dad!

### Track 8

ZOOKEEPER: This lion is very big and strong now. But he used to be small! A baby lion is called a cub. This lion used to play all the time. But now he sleeps a lot!
ALEX BLACK: He's just like my cat! She didn't use to sleep all day. She used to play all the time when she was a baby.
ZOOKEEPER: Do you know what a baby cat is called?
ALEX BLACK: A baby cat is called a kitten.
ZOOKEEPER: Yes! Did you know that baby rabbits are called kittens, too?
ALEX BLACK: Really? No, I didn't know that.

### Track 9

**Life Used to Be So Good**

I used to go to the beach.
I used to play in the sand,
I used to swim in the sea,
My friends used to go with me.

Chorus:
I used to do it, but now I don't.
Life used to be so good!
I used to do it, but now I don't.
This year I really should!

I used to stay in hotels,
They used to have a big pool.
I used to lie in the sun,
I used to have lots of fun.

(Chorus)

I used to surf the big waves.
I used to collect white shells,
I used to sail in a boat,
Now it all seems so remote.

(Chorus)

## Unit 4

### Track 10

FATHER: Isn't this trip exciting? I love traveling by car!
3 GIRLS: Well… / Okay… / Uhmm…
FATHER: Yesterday, we traveled 200 miles. Today, we're traveling 250 miles. And tomorrow, we're going to travel 300 miles!
3 GIRLS: Are we there yet? Are we there yet? Are we there yet?

### Track 11

ANGELA: How was your weekend?
VICKY: It was wonderful! On Friday, I went shopping and bought a beautiful dress. On Saturday, I put on my new dress and went dancing. And on Sunday, I went sailing on the lake! How about you?
ANGELA: On Friday, I went swimming, but I caught a cold. So on Saturday and Sunday, I stayed home and slept!
VICKY: I'm sorry! I hope you feel better soon!

### Track 12

**New York, New York**

On September 21st, I'm going to fly to New York.
I'm going to travel alone; I'm sure I'm going to have fun.

Chorus:
New York, New York, it's a wonderful place to be.
That Big Red Apple is going to welcome me.

I'm going to see the sights; I'm going to walk all day long.
I'm going to buy some postcards; I'm going to send them to you.

(Chorus)

I'm going to buy souvenirs; I'm going to go to the zoo.
I'm going to take a night tour; I'm never going to go home.

(Chorus)

I'm going to eat hamburgers; I'm going to watch new movies.
I'm going to shop in Soho; I'm going to buy gifts for you.

(Chorus)

## Unit 5

### Track 13

BOY: What a perfect street for skateboarding! I can go faster, and faster, and faster… Wheee!
MAN: What a big, heavy box of eggs! Oof! I can't see around it!
MAN: Ugh! Eggs everywhere!
BOY: You should watch where you're going!
MAN: Well, you shouldn't ride so fast!

### Track 14

JAMES: Hello, nurse. You have to help me.
NURSE: What's the matter?
JAMES: I have a terrible stomachache!
NURSE: Why?
JAMES: Because I entered a pie-eating contest, and I won!
NURSE: Oh, dear. You shouldn't eat a lot of pie all at once.
JAMES: I had to eat a lot to win! But now my stomach really hurts.
NURSE: You should take this medicine to help your stomach. But you mustn't eat so much pie again!
JAMES: I know now! Thanks, nurse.

### Track 15

**We Have to, We Should**

Chorus:
We have to, we have to, we have to do
Everything our teachers tell us to.
We have to, we have to, we have to do
Everything our parents tell us to.

You should go to school.
You should learn the rule.
You shouldn't jump in the pool.
You shouldn't be a fool!

(Chorus)

You should help at home.
You should use the comb.
You shouldn't stay alone.
You shouldn't talk on the phone!

(Chorus)

You should never be mean.
You should eat your green beans.
You shouldn't leave your team.
You shouldn't yell or scream!

(Chorus)

## Unit 6

### Track 16

BOY: Mom, will it be sunny at the beach this afternoon?
MOM: Wait. Let's listen!
RADIO WEATHER FORECASTER: And a good morning to everyone out there! It looks like it'll be a sunny day by the sea! And in other weather news…
MOM: Yes, it will be sunny! That's what the weather forecast on the radio says.
BOY: Wow, this is great!
MOM: Hmm… Is that a cloud in the sky?
BOY: Oh no!
MOM: Quick – under the umbrella!!
BOY: Mom, will you listen to that weather forecast next time?
MOM: No, I won't!

### Track 17

MARY: Where will we go for the holidays?
MOM: We'll go to Grandma's house at the beach.
MARY: Wow! What will we do there?
MOM: We'll swim and lie on the sand.
MARY: What will we wear?
MOM: It'll be hot, so we'll wear swimsuits and shorts!
MARY: That will be fun. Here everyone will be wearing winter coats!

### Track 18

(See page 63.)

## Unit 7

### Track 19

DAD: This is the place where I work. Welcome to "Bring–Your–Children–to–Work Day," kids!
BRIAN: Thanks, Dad. Hey, Dave, run over there and catch this football!
DAVE: I caught it, Brian! Race you across the office!
DAD: Boys! Stop! Well, this is usually the place where I work. But today, it's the place where they play…

### Track 20

BILL: Let's plan our day. What should we do?
JILL: Let's do our homework first. Then we won't make mistakes because we're in a hurry.
BILL: Okay. Next, let's do the chores. But we don't have to make the bed because I already did.
JILL: Thanks! Then, let's eat lunch. I'll make our food…
BILL: And I'll do the dishes afterward.
JILL: Great! Finally, let's do something fun.
BILL: Okay. We can make a craft or do a puzzle!

### Track 21
**Instructions**

Chorus:
Instructions here,
Instructions there.
I see instructions everywhere.

First, plug the toaster in.
Then, put the bread inside.
Next, watch those slices burn.
They said it worked. They lied!

(Chorus)

First, pour some milk in the blender.
Then, add some sugar, a lot.
Next, turn the speed to *high*.
Oops, I forgot the top!

(Chorus)

First, put the batteries in.
Then, turn the radio on.
Next, find the station you like.
Come on, sing your favorite song!

## Unit 8

### Track 22

MOM: Adam, please walk the dog.
ADAM: Okay, Mom.
MOM: Adam, what are you doing? Why are all the ducks running around?
ADAM: You wanted me to walk the ducks. Look, they're getting lots of exercise!
MOM: Oh dear. No, Adam, I asked you to walk the *dog*, not the *ducks*!
ADAM: Ohhh!

### Track 23

JILL: I really like our new TV, Mom!
MOM: Me, too! Let's watch something. Please turn it on.
JILL: Nothing's happening. Should I shake it?
MOM: No, never shake a TV.
JILL: Should we take it back to the store?
MOM: Hmm… let's read the instructions carefully.
JILL: Okay. Here they are. "First, plug it in."
MOM: Oh! I forgot! There. Try it again.
JILL: Great! It's working much better now!

### Track 24
**Up and Far Away**

Look up at the big black sky.
Come with me and we can fly.
We can see Earth from far away:
See the change from night to day.

Chorus:
An astronaut says:
"See you soon!
My space ship
Is ready to go
To the moon."

Planet Jupiter is big and old,
And Mars is red and cold.
Satellites travel all over the place,
And bring us news from outer space.

(Chorus)

# Vocabulary